Author of the books
Prayer and *Knowing the Holy Spirit*

FASTING &
PRAYER

FOUNDATIONS FOR DEEP WORSHIP
AND LETHAL SPIRITUAL WARFARE.

PASTOR NNAEMEKA C. UCHEGBU

FASTING & PRAYER

FOUNDATIONS FOR DEEP WORSHIP AND LETHAL SPIRITUAL WARFARE.

iUniverse books may be ordered through booksellers or by contacting:

iUniverse
1663 Liberty Drive
Bloomington, IN 47403
www.iuniverse.com
844-349-9409

Because of the dynamic nature of the Internet, any web addresses or links contained in this book may have changed since publication and may no longer be valid. The views expressed in this work are solely those of the author and do not necessarily reflect the views of the publisher, and the publisher hereby disclaims any responsibility for them.

Any people depicted in stock imagery provided by Getty Images are models, and such images are being used for illustrative purposes only. Certain stock imagery © Getty Images.

Scripture quotations are from the Holy Bible, King james Version (Authorized Version). First published in 1611. Quoted from the KJV Classic Reference Bible, Copyright 1983 by The Zondervan Corporation.

ISBN: 978-1-6632-2855-0 (sc)
ISBN: 978-1-6632-2856-7 (e)

Library of Congress Control Number: 2021918145

Print information available on the last page.

iUniverse rev. date: 09/13/2021

CONTENTS

CONTENTS

DEDICATED TO:

My dear wife Yikimwapet Faith, the
bright star in my dark cloud.

My four wonderful children: Chizomam,
Kelechi, Sharon and Divine. My
invaluable rewards from the Lord.

My lovely daughter-in-law: Adesola-
Kelechi. A godly addition to my family.

And my bubbly, first granddaughter: Grace.
The "Genesis" of greater things to come.

ACKNOWLEDGEMENT

I deeply acknowledge my daughter in the Lord, Sister Magaret Tolbert, and my good friend, Pastor Anselm Jibunor. Your financial assistance helped make this book a reality.

My deep appreciation to all our awesome Pastors, the Ministers, Sunday-school teachers, Board members and entire congregation of Amazing Grace Ministries. Your encouragement has been very wonderful.

And to my brilliant "editor in the house", Pastor Bruno; thank you for patiently reading through the manuscript and correcting the errors.

May the amazing God we serve, in his amazing grace, do amazing things, in amazing ways, in all your lives.

FOREWORD

The book, "Fasting and Prayer", is an eye opener. It unequivocally shows how to be rich for God, strong in prayer and become unbeatable for the foes of your souls through biblical fasting and praying. It is a spiritual guidepost for those who are resolute to get rid of every satanic manipulation and orchestration over their lives.

By the title of the book, it is not difficult to conclude that, fasting is not optional for those who want to win the battles of life, it is a compulsion.

Out of his many years of Christian journey and wealth of ministerial experiences, the author enlightens every reader what a biblical fasting is, gives some useful and helpful hints on Christian fasting and analyzed the power that resides in combining prayer with fasting.

In the book, the author has equally done justice to clearing the air about some myths attached to fasting. Also, he touched issues on the power of a Christian or biblical fasting.

This material is therefore more than a book. It is a message to the world and an energy booster to all believers in Christ. It is recommended for every intending victor as a must read for all and sundry. Every serious-minded Christian desiring to walk with God and work for God must read it over and again.

In short, those who read this must not just keep it but give to others to read and make it their companion and compass. With this, you can easily navigate through the wilderness of life and sail easily to your promised land. Be blessed as you read!

Rev. Dr. Kayode Ayinde
Senior Pastor,
First Baptist Church,
Ado Ekiti, Ekiti State,
Nigeria.

INTRODUCTION

The knowledge of God's word is, indeed, very beneficial to every aspect of the believer's life. But in the end, what matters is not how much of it was known, but how this word was applied by anyone, not only in his own life, but in influencing the lives of other people for God.

God's word is rich with spiritual assets. And the individual who acquires, and wisely applies these mysteries in his life will soundly enjoy a beneficial relationship with God. The Devil understands this quite well and will do all he can to ensure that such rapport does not exist.

Prayer and fasting are two of the most significant spiritual assets available to God's children for establishing a relationship with him and in dealing with the unending battles of life. So, any Christian who desires to enjoy victories in life and have good success must be skilled with them.

However, while prayer is the very commonly applied instrument in all religious circles, the concept of fasting, is sadly not in vogue with many believers. People who readily and routinely pray anytime and in any place, will scarcely engage in a fast.

In so doing, many Christians deny themselves the best means of approaching the throne of mercy and grace. As a result, they miss the privileges of God's divine presence where gifts and mysteries reserved for those who diligently seek God are dispensed.

It is undeniable that prayer is a great tool of communication in the quest for friendship and fellowship with God, and a powerful weapon of warfare. But Jesus, the greatest prayer warrior that ever lived, did not rely only on prayer.

He explained to his disciples that there were conditions, both in the spiritual and natural realms, that demanded more than prayer alone could handle. And to adequately deal with such situations, he taught them to apply a combination of prayer and fasting.

Yet, despite this revelation and the fact that it is even practiced in several cultures and across all religions, not many Christians readily identify with taming the instinctive appetite for foods and drinks for sacred reasons. Only very few summon the courage to do so.

To the human flesh, fasting is an unwelcome resetting of the basic instincts that help it to survive. So, the flesh tends to resist this great, lethal weapon, which is an inevitable spiritual tool, especially for those believers who desire spiritual growth.

The habitual lust for foods and drinks, the cravings for sugar, and other human addictions, is what makes fasting appear touch. But the ease about fasting comes with practice and prayer. When a believer resolves to spend such time with God, the Holy Spirit provides the strength.

Also, when fasting is combined with fervent prayers based on God's word, the result is an amazing perception into his divine presence and the revelation of his power. This combination increases the believer's faith and readily reminds him of God's ability to deliver.

Christians who are proficient with these tools, appreciate that when they are combined in worship or spiritual warfare, they generate unusual power that can change things in the atmosphere, both in heaven and on earth. That is why it is important for Christians to fast and pray regularly.

This book, along with many others that have been written on this subject matter will help such committed believers to understand the many acceptable ways a combined fasting and prayer program can benefit their lives.

Therefore, as someone who has enjoyed these benefits, I have written this book as my own contribution to demystify the many general beliefs that these disciplines are reserved only for priests, prophets, and pastors, or for those who are in trouble.

So, as you read through its chapters, I pray that you find out for yourself whether this is true or false. And if your findings are helpful in anyway, give all the credit to the Holy Spirit who is the great revealer of all things.

I hope you will find this book interesting.

CHAPTER ONE

WHAT IS A RELIGIOUS FAST?

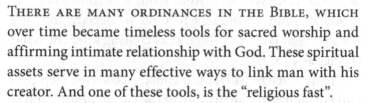

THERE ARE MANY ORDINANCES IN THE BIBLE, WHICH over time became timeless tools for sacred worship and affirming intimate relationship with God. These spiritual assets serve in many effective ways to link man with his creator. And one of these tools, is the "religious fast".

A fast is a voluntary process of abstaining from physical foods and or liquids for religious reasons. It is a way through which a soul that is hungry for spiritual growth abandons what the world offers, to possess what God provides, thereby finding deep friendship with God.

It is a time of seclusion that enables the mind to wholly engage in deep meaningful communication with God. During this process, the soul pours out its sorrow to God allowing the heaviness in his broken heart to be offloaded before the creator of the universe (Matthew 11: 28).

A fast provides the believer ample time to sincerely worship God, genuinely confess one's sins and the sins of others, and repent of them. It offers the proper atmosphere to ask for God's forgiveness and mercy, and to seek his help.

It is a time when one is alone with God, just to let him know how sufficient he is for all his needs. This is when a believer employs valuable time to express utter dependence on the faithful God, who is his great provider.

A genuine fast is one which involves the declaration of man's total inability to find meaning and completion in a life without God. It exposes the folly and arrogance of the immoral soul which makes the carnal man to imagine that he can live his life without God.

A religious fast is a somber moment when a man submits, in total humility, to acknowledge that everything he is and can ever be, is from God. It is time when the subdued mind surrenders to God to declare that life without God is as meaningless as chasing after the wind (Ecclesiastes 3: 11).

Thus, a religious fast is a conscious, sacred step by a child of God to purge his soul of the carnal desires of life, and thereby enable his spirit to possess what God has in stock. It is a sacrifice that a believer makes to be more like Christ.

This exercise along with other disciplines such as prayer, studying and meditating in God's word, combine to build the solid platform for intimate fellowship with God. A Christian that is committed to genuine fasts will no doubt be a good friend of Jesus.

"And he took with him Peter and the two sons of Zebedee and began to be sorrowful and very heavy. Then saith he unto them, My soul is exceeding sorrowful, even unto death: tarry ye here, and watch with me." (Matthew 26: 37-38).

Fasting results in the mental shift that enables a Christian to set his mind wholly on God. It is a means whereby the malnourished soul and spirit reach out to God for necessary refreshment. The person who desires to be in the mold of Christ must live by selfless denial and sacrifice.

The consistency of prayer, commitment of faith, selfless sacrifice and denial of fleshly desires combine to keep a person spiritually fit for God. All these factors come into play during a fast and help the believer to seal any cracks in his relationship with God through Christ.

A religious fast provides occasion for a Christian to mourn for his human errors and to make amends. A Christian who fasts regularly will hate sin. He is aware of his eternal destination and will be cautious to maintain a righteous state of mind. (1 Corinthians 6: 9-11).

Fasting is the believer's humble way of reaffirming loyalty, trust, humility, and confidence in God. This way, that person acknowledges the weakness of his humanity while honestly expressing the reality of his need for God.

And Jesus said unto them, Can the children of the bridechamber mourn, as long as the bridegroom is with them? but the days will come, when the bridegroom shall be taken from them, and then shall they fast. (Matthew 9: 15).

A fast is a statute ordained by God to enable his children to engage in inter-personal encounters, experience un-interruptible fellowship, and enjoy exclusive communion with him. This enables the human spirit to come into sweet union with the spirit of his maker.

The religious fast is the believer's practical way of developing his spiritual, faith muscles. Faith is necessary for dealing with spiritual issues like fear, worry and temptations that target the mind. A fasted soul is always on the alert and will not succumb to these weapons of the Devil.

A fast involves the resting of the body to enable the hurting and heavily burdened soul to heal. It helps the soul to vomit any lingering deposits of anger, bitterness, hate and pride so that the spirit can be filled with love, kindness, patience, and compassion.

Religious fasting is the deliberate effort by man to walk away from the seductions of this carnal world to enable the human soul to seek the awesome presence of God. It is a move by the natural man to explore the spirit realm so that he can find, or refresh intimacy with God.

A genuine fasting regimen is the appropriate time to bring critical human needs before the throne of a compassionate God in a way that prayer alone cannot adequately present them. It is a time for the deep cry against long standing problems that defy solutions.

Fasting is established in the Bible as a practical means for keeping a man's relationship with God active. The more regular and effective a Christian's fasting life is, the closer his spirit is to God, the farther away from problems and the easier to address them if they arise.

Fasting is one major way of preparing the believer for effective spiritual warfare. It equips Christians with the knowledge and power for handling the agenda of the wicked, dismantling the activities of demons, and rendering their weapons powerless.

Fasting results in the weakening of the human flesh as his spirit is strengthened. That begins with the feeding of the spirit with the word of God while the flesh is denied any natural desires. This way, the spirit of a man is enabled to work in harmony with the Spirit of God.

This intentional denial of natural foods and liquids to the human body, while at the same time feeding the soul and spirit with spiritual food help to build the believer's faith. It makes him ready for handling temptation and everything that appears as sin.

It helps to shape a believer's spiritual lifestyle. This is crucial for those who desire to develop a strong spirit that the enemy cannot manipulate, seduce, or confuse. It also ensures the formation of good moral characters.

Fasting helps a believer to find himself in the presence of God. And before the throne of grace, the Christian will obtain mercy and favors. In this spiritual mode he will be blessed with uncommon, divine goodness and gifts for ministry.

"As they ministered to the Lord, and fasted, the Holy Ghost said, separate me Barnabas and Saul for the work whereunto I have called them. And when they had fasted and prayed, and laid their hands on them, they sent them away." (Acts 13: 2—3).

Religious fasting helps in understanding and appreciating spiritual things. It does not only reveal the secrets of heaven to the totally obedient Christian but prepares his heart to make necessary sacrifices in arears that set him apart for use in God's kingdom.

The process of fasting will lift a Christian's soul to the realm where he is no longer affected by the lusts of his flesh, or controlled by emotional vices such as envy, pride, jealousy, and hate. In this state, the soul has no reason to covet any evil.

Anytime spent fasting will help the soul of a Christian repair itself from the damages of sin and to heal the wounds inflicted on the mind by a perverted world. This is when that believer can focus on the things that bring him lasting joy and godly peace.

Fasting is an amazing way of bringing the best out of a person's character. This explains why most great men and women of the Bible used this sacred platform while they built their relationships with God. Prophet Daniel was one such people.

"In the third year of Cyrus king of Persia a thing was revealed unto Daniel, whose name was called Belteshazzar; and the thing was true, but the time appointed was long: and he understood the thing, and had understanding of the vision. In those days I Daniel was mourning three full weeks. I ate no pleasant bread, neither came flesh nor wine in my mouth, neither did I anoint myself at all, till three whole weeks were fulfilled. And in the four and twentieth day of the first month, as I was by the side of the great river, which is Hiddekel; Then I lifted up mine eyes, and looked, and behold a certain man clothed in linen, whose loins were girded with fine gold of Uphaz:" (Daniel 10: 1-5)

"And he said unto me, O Daniel, a man greatly beloved, understand the words that I speak unto thee, and stand upright: for unto thee am I now sent. And when he had spoken this word unto me, I stood trembling.

Then said he unto me, Fear not, Daniel: for from the first day that thou didst set thine heart to understand, and to chasten thyself before thy God, thy words were heard, and I am come for thy words." (Daniel 10: 11-12).

Daniel was a prayer warrior who had firm faith in the Sovereign God and understood the necessity of fasts. But his enemies conspired, and convinced king Nebuchadnezzar to throw him into the den of lions because he would not bow to the king's idol. But God delivered him.

Another time, many years after this horrible experience, he fasted and prayed, pleading with God for the deliverance of his Jewish people, after they had spent seventy years in captivity. Thereafter, God answered him through a vision.

Fasting changes things, and believers can turn the course of history around by relying on this asset. Daniel's twenty-one days fast attracted the swift visitation of an angel. Heaven responded to his requests and rewarded him with a message that people around him could not hear.

God grants his goodness to people who reaffirm their confidence in him, his Son, and the Holy Spirit. And he is good to all disciplined souls who willingly do his will and completely obey his commandment without grumbling. (Lamentations 3: 25)

Fasting helps the heart and the mind to conform to spiritual rules in ways that are in harmony with divine laws. It provides a faithful believer the chance to develop a Christlike mindset and thereby have the time to worship God with an attitude of thanksgiving.

As a person denies the body natural foods and liquids, his organs are freed up to eliminate toxins that cause sickness in body. And as junk foods are replaced with the refreshing word of God, the human spirit is regenerated, the soul renewed and the body repairs naturally.

A strong child of God is a person that is healthy in the spirit, soul and in the body. This kind of believer can face sudden trials without fear when they come. Such people are filled with strength ahead of time to deal with life's challenges.

Every one that is alive will encounter challenges that are both natural and spiritual in nature. And because all spiritual problems come from the Devil, every Christian needs to train himself in the art of fasting and prayer and be thoroughly equipped for the day of trouble.

When that time comes, carnal weapons will not do the job. Jesus the Son of God understood this clearly. So, he fasted for forty days and nights to prepare himself for his ministry. This helped him overcome the temptations he faced in the wilderness and thereafter.

The habit of fasting and chastening the soul is a great method for training in spiritual warfare. It is the best way to equip the human spirit with spiritual weapons and to prepare the soul for the inevitable trials of life.

The Bible demands that Christians regularly engage in fasts and admonishes them to pray ceaselessly. So, fasting is a mandate that should not be considered as an option, but a necessity in the life of any believer who desires to experience constant victories in life.

There are good chances of a person hearing from God during a fast and receiving mysteries that he would not reveal to the ordinary mind. As a person's spirit pleases God, he will order his feet aright and gladly reveal secrets of his kingdom to him.

"Call unto me, and I will answer thee, and show thee great and mighty things, which thou knowest not" (Jeremiah 33: 3).

Fasting will endow a child of God with strength for troubled times. So, the implication for not fasting is the loss of spiritual power, wisdom and many other privileges reserved for those that regularly and selflessly make this sacrificial.

The objective of fasting is to restore a person's spiritual mind-set. During the process, the soul focuses on more gainful spiritual realities, rather than on the fruitless, carnal habits, worldly leisure, and practices that destroy the soul and the body.

Fasting is the best spiritual technique for building friendship with God. And in that friendly atmosphere, anyone can boldly reason with God as a child will reason with his earthly father. This provides the good opportunity to cultivate sensitivity to his voice.

"Come now, and let us reason together, saith the LORD: *though your sins be as scarlet, they shall be as white as snow; though they be red like crimson, they shall be as wool" (Isaiah 1: 18).*

It is every believer's privilege to take up words in appreciation of the almighty God. But sadly, this is not achievable in our overcrowded and noisy society. So, only those few Christians who regularly set time aside to fast and pray, enjoy the blessings of God's presence.

It is in the presence of the sovereign creator of all things that godly character is learned and virtuous habits that enable fruitful relationship with the father of all flesh is developed. That is why, those who desire to bear meaningful fruit God's kingdom love to tarry there.

Every genuine religious fast is a beneficial walk into the secret place of the Most-High God. It is the place where the poor find protection and needy are secured with strength. There also, those who are in distress find comfort and refuge.

Wonderful things happen in God's presence. So, a Christian who invests valuable time to fast and pray, and humbly seeks the face of God, will receive useful instructions for ministry. He will grow in spiritual dimensions above others who do not have this habit.

"Now there were in the church that was at Antioch certain prophets and teachers; as Barnabas, and Simeon that was called Niger, and Lucius of Cyrene, and Manaen, which had been brought up with Herod the tetrarch, and Saul. As they ministered to the Lord, and fasted, the Holy Ghost said, Separate me Barnabas and Saul for the work whereunto I have called them" (Acts 13: 2).

A fast is a life-changing experience that brings rewards from God. It is a timeless symbol of surrender to God, good evidence of complete dependence on him and a great sacred platform for reiterating sacrificial faith and humility.

It is a good time for a person to humbly present his spirit before God, to chasten his soul in his presence and to weep there in repentance of one's sins. This will help that Christian with the opportunity to find forgiveness, grace, and mercy.

A Christian that will commit to fasting and prayer, exclusive of his normal "quite time with God", will notice a great change in his life. God wants to transform lives. And he will gladly choose from those he finds, afflicting their souls, on the altar of fasting and prayer.

PRAYER POINTS

1. O Lord, open the door of your awesome presence to me, as I fast and pray, in Jesus' name.

2. My father, as I fast and pray, cause the dew of your favor to settle upon my life, in Jesus' name.

3. My God, let the aroma of my prayers in this fast become like sweet-smelling incense to you, in Jesus' name.

4. O God, let my prayers in this fast become like hammer and break every agreement with death, in Jesus' name.

5. As I fast and pray, blood of Jesus, cancel the appointment with death, scheduled for me in the coven, in Jesus' name.

6. My Father, as I fast and pray, increase me where the enemy has concluded plans to diminish me, in Jesus' name.

7. Holy Spirit, reveal something new to me, as I fast and pray, in Jesus' name.

8. Holy Spirit, draw me closer to the heart of God as I fast and pray, in Jesus' name.

9. O God that sees in secret, honor my humble fast and prayers, in Jesus' name.

10. Holy Spirit, help me to find God's will as I fast and pray, in Jesus' name.

11. Holy Spirit, as I fast and pray, help me to do God's will, in Jesus' name.

12. Holy Spirit, make my matter to matter before God, in this my fasting and prayer program, in Jesus' name.

13. Blood of Jesus become my healing tonic as I fast and pray, in Jesus' name.

14. Evil yokes operating in my life, be broken to pieces, as I fast and pray, in Jesus' name.

CHAPTER TWO

TYPES OF FASTING

A RELIGIOUS FAST IS A SACRED EXERCISE THAT HAS MANY purposes. Some of these purposes include the desire for spiritual growth, which can be helpful in dealing with spiritual challenges, emotional situations, moral issues, and physical trials.

Another useful purpose of a fast is the role it plays in developing a disciplined way of life. This type of lifestyle reflects holiness, enhances righteous habits, and keeps believers in line with thoughts, imaginations and deeds that are pleasant to God.

And, because the purposes of a fast vary, it can take many forms.

For this reason, different persons in the Bible adopted various forms that suited their underlying motives. And notwithstanding their choice, God answered them respectively, according to his will.

So, it is re-assuring to observe how God responds to the sacrifices of a contrite spirit and a broken heart. When human sacrifices find acceptance before God, he rewards the people involved, not because of the format of worship, but for their acts love and selflessness.

BIBLICAL FASTING

A fast is a sacred discipline of worship approved in the Bible. And while religious fasts have different variations, there are characteristics that are common to all the forms. These include the deliberate or willful abstention from foods, liquids, sex, and the desire to help the needy.

Engaging in any one or a combination of these things during a fast is considered as an expression of human loyalty and submission to God. It represents a declaration of the supremacy of God over all other gods and idols.

Biblical fasting is a man's pleasant way of appreciating God who by his grace chose his human body as his temple. So, denying the flesh its carnal desires, for a time, just to nourish it with spiritual food, is an acceptable sacrifice that honors God.

But as serious as the fasting mandate is for all believers, there is no specific guideline for it in the Bible. Thus, except for the once a year, "Day of Atonement" fast stated in the Torah, the pattern for any religious fast is dictated by individual or group goals.

"It shall be unto you a sabbath of rest, and ye shall afflict your souls: in the ninth day of the month at even, from even unto even, shall ye celebrate your sabbath" (Leviticus 23: 32).

This open-ended nature of a fast is the reason there are different types. So, while Moses, Elijah and Jesus fasted for 40-days respectively, Daniel fasted for 21-days. And others like Queen Esther, apostles Paul, Peter and the early disciples fasted for about three days in a row.

15

The abstention from foods, luxuries, and all other comforts during the Jewish feast of Atonement was mandatory in the Law of Moses. But in addition to this, the Pharisees fasted two extra days every week. This was their way of expressing extra religious piety.

Jesus was critical of this practice by the Pharisees, and he seriously condemned such outward acts of self-righteousness which were done to gain human praise. For this reason, the Bible encourages a process that is done secretly, sincerely and from a humble heart.

In the Old Testament period, different Jewish religious sects fasted for different reasons. And the religious observances by these religious groups varied from each other. Their respective doctrines determined the modalities.

While some fasting demanded total abstention from food and water (Esther 4:16), others followed strict dietary restrictions (Daniel 10:3). In one instance, both humans and beasts were mandated by the King to go without food and water for days. (Jonah 3:7-9)

There were no time limits for individual fasts in the Bible. But the duration and schedules were dictated by individual circumstances, human needs, spiritual conditions of a nation, or as required by specific religious cultures.

In the Bible, nations that feared God fasted when they came under his chastisement. Kings fasted before battle, and sinners chastened their souls in repentance. Others fasted when in need, in danger, in times of spiritual conflict and in desperation. Even the church fasted.

"As they ministered to the Lord, and fasted, the Holy Ghost said, Separate me Barnabas and Saul for the work whereunto I have called them. And when they had fasted and prayed, and laid their hands on them, they sent them away" (Acts 13: 2-3).

Biblical fasting is one mark of spiritual surrender that will revive the human spirit, strengthen a person's faith in Christ and reaffirm his relationship with God. It is undoubtedly a reliable path to staying pure and undefiled amid a perverse world.

It is a secure way of spiritual refreshment which also protects the soul in times of emotional crisis. A mind that is spiritually stable will avoid the worldly seductions marketed via the internet, the television, and the telephone.

Biblical fasting is a believer's most dependable way of staying in touch with God. It opens an underserved lifeline of grace to all who deny their flesh of all the worldly attractions just to feed their soul with God's holy word and be in his presence.

"My flesh and my heart faileth: but God is the strength of my heart, and my portion forever" (Psalm 73: 26).

"I will lift up mine eyes unto the hills, from whence cometh my help. My help cometh from the LORD, which made heaven and earth" (Psalm 121: 1-2).

As much as God desires regular worship from his children, he still demands that such an act be selfless and deliberate. Thus, a child of God who desires to go on a fast must genuinely approach it in a willful spirit. This is the fast that delights God's heart.

In a world cancerously infected by systemic racism, insane cultural and religious biases, all creation seems to be standing on the brink of hell. But as Christians fast and pray, the love of Christ can permeate the world so that all can leave at peace, without prejudice for one another.

PRIVATE FASTING

There is much evidence in the Bible showing that private fasting was practiced in the Old Testament period. It served then as a measure to strengthen personal relationship with God. It also inspired hope among believers in ways that kept biblical promises alive and realistic.

And following suit in the New Testament, believers also adopted this pattern of worship because of the privacy it offered. So, not only do priests, pastors, and servants in the house of God engage in private fasts, ordinary faithful souls also use the method.

Every human creature at some stage in life will face a measure of spiritual warfare. And when that time comes, only spiritually disciplined believers, trained in the use of spiritual weapons will survive the test. Fasting is one of those weapons.

Personal or individual fasts help build the believer's readiness to cope in times of adverse situations. It helps the Christian to recalibrate his spiritual mindset causing him to remain focused on doing the will of God.

Daniel was a prayer warrior who without doubt engaged in all the stipulated fasts of Judaism. So, on arrival in Babylon as slaves, he and his three friends embarked on a ten-day fast. They stayed away from the king's food and lived only on vegetables and water.

After ten days of such sacrifice, they looked better in appearance than their contemporaries. God further blessed them in learning, spiritual understanding, wisdom, and skills which turned the keen attention of the King's chief of staff on them.

As a result, Daniel was drafted to be a counsellor in the royal court of King Nebuchadnezzar. And with God's help, he continued to enjoy uncommon favor before the King. So, even as a slave in the kingdom of Babylon, fasting positioned Daniel for divine elevation.

The royal language of the Babylonians was Aramaic. And the crash academic program that Daniel went through must have included mathematics, and astronomy. He would also have been exposed to the magic of the Chaldeans. But his fasts kept him focused on God.

As a result, God gave him exceeding favor and he excelled above his peers in the land of Babylon. During private fasts, a believer finds himself in seclusion where the Holy Spirit will guide, strengthen, and uphold him as he is nourished by God's word.

Any child of God engaged in a private fast will find himself in an atmosphere that will enable his spirit to connect with the Spirit of God. In this mode the Christian can obtain instructions for specific directions and embrace the humility to do the will of God.

A Private fast will bring a person's soul to a sacred place where God's voice can be clearly heard without doubts or distractions. And the humble surrender involved during such sessions will crush emotions of fear, pride, and selfishness, leaving room for peace and clarity of mind.

INTERMITENT FAST.

Many believers sadly find it difficult, for certain personal reasons, to practice the regular, time framed, fasting. Some people, for instance, avoid fasting for obvious health issues, while others skip it because the nature of their career would not grant them the time to do it.

But Christians who know the benefits of a fast will practice it regularly. That is why some choose the intermittent fasting method to ensure that they do not lose completely from the priceless rewards and tremendous benefits of this sacred mandate.

While the Bible does not condemn intermittent fasting, it is certain that no one can receive the Moses' anointing or glory by this method. And the history of the Fathers of the faith who operated in high spiritual anointing will not be complete without the price they paid for it.

They all made uncommon sacrifice for the great power that rested on them. And that power was not gained through the intermittent fast. However, it is not impossible, that both Moses and Jesus would also have practiced the intermittent fast during their ministry.

FORTY-DAYS FAST.

Not all children of God can fast like Moses, Elijah, or Jesus. These characters fasted for forty days and nights single sessions respectively. No wonder the anointing of God upon them was incredible. This was what made their ministries unique.

It is on record that Moses fasted for forty days and forty nights on Mount Sinai, before he received the Law from God. This was not just a one-off thing. Because he deliberately embarked on this type fast on two other occasions.

In the gospel of Matthew, it is specifically stated that Jesus fasted for forty days and forty nights too, before he launched his ministry. It is an incredible human feat for the natural man to go without food and, or water for that length of time.

"And when he had fasted forty days and forty nights, he was afterward an hungred." (Matthew 4: 2)

Naturally, the body is not supposed to starve for a long time. While it can cope without food and liquids for about ten to twenty-one days, the human organs will begin to shut down thereafter. And if God does not intervene, this can lead to shock and ultimately to death.

That is why many believers settle for the less tasking, intermittent method. And while there is nothing wrong with that type of a fast, it may not bring the level of spiritual power and clarity of mind that Moses, Elijah and Jesus obtained after their 40-day fasts.

It has its benefits and rewards. And those who are blessed to make it to the end have no regrets. No fasting method can discipline the soul or finetune the mind like it. Unfortunately, only few people can keep up with this type of fast.

PUBLIC FASTING

In the Old Testament era, fasting was a common religious practice. Generally, public fasts were proclaimed to seek divine favor, to chasten the soul, before any war, to plead for God's intervention during a season of famine and drought, or as a sign of national repentance.

"And they gathered together to Mizpeh, and drew water, and poured it out before the LORD, and fasted on that day, and said there, We have sinned against the LORD. And Samuel judged the children of Israel in Mizpeh." (1Samuel 7:6).

It came to pass after this also, that the children of Moab, and the children of Ammon, and with them other beside the Ammonites, came against Jehoshaphat to battle. Then there came some that told Jehoshaphat, saying, There cometh a great multitude against thee from beyond the sea on this side Syria; and, behold, they be in Hazazon-tamar, which is En-gedi. And Jehoshaphat feared, and set himself to seek the LORD, and proclaimed a fast throughout all Judah. (2 Chronicles 20:1-3).

As part of the Mosaic law, fasting was a statutory requirement for the nation of Israel as commanded by God. It was not an ordinary human suggestion. Thus, whenever the people humbled themselves as a nation, and fasted, God responded to their request.

The story of the exiles who returned from the Babylonian captivity under the leadership of Ezra the Scribe, is a good illustration of the role of a fast in the life of a nation. So, for the children of Israel, fasting was not just a religious pattern but a national lifestyle.

The returnees under Ezra were mainly women, aged priests, and defenseless children. They brought along many of the precious articles of worship, traveling through approximately nine hundred miles of harsh terrains and dangerous zones often patrolled by highway robbers.

But Ezra understood the high risk of this trip. He realized ahead of the trip that the task was going to be tough. So, before they set out, he called for a public fast. The objective was to seek for God's guidance and protection.

"Then I proclaimed a fast there, at the river of Ahava, that we might afflict ourselves before our God, to seek of him a right way for us, and for our little ones, and for all our substance. For I was ashamed to require of the king a band of soldiers and horsemen to help us against the enemy in the way: because we had spoken unto the king, saying, The hand of our God is upon all them for good that seek him; but his power and his wrath is against all them that forsake him. So we fasted and besought our God for this: and he was intreated of us (Ezra 8: 21-23).

Ezra had the option of asking for royal escorts. But he had boasted of the protection of the arm of God that protects his people. So, when the situation arose to lead the returnee exiles on that forty-month journey by foot, he called for a fast. And God answered them favorably.

Public fasts, general fasts and group fasts are the same. They can be used by a church congregation, a believing cultural community or a nation. It is always a great idea to make spiritual preparations ahead of all physical plans. It worked for Ezra, and it will work for you.

SELECTIVE INDIVIDUAL FASTS.

There are specific cases in the Bible where individuals adopted this kind of fasting. In selective fast, the individual involved determines to fast every day. What they do is to eat only one meal at a particular time and never eat again till the next day.

For a Christian who decides to follow this pattern of fasting and prayer, the choice is a personal one. And if the sacrifice made during the process helps that person to focus his attention on God and accomplish other godly motives, it will still be acceptable as a fast.

Anna was a prophetess in the Bible who practiced this form of fast. Although she was eighty-four years old, she had lived in the temple since the early days of her widowhood, serving God with fastings and prayers, because she hoped to see the Messiah (Luke 2: 36-37).

FORCED FASTING.

Nineveh was a powerful and prosperous city of about one hundred and seventy-five thousand people at the time of Jonah. But there was sin and much wickedness in that land. The inhabitants of the Nineveh were vile and relished in unprecedented level of atrocities.

They were known for their fierceness in battle, and were partly responsible for the instability, hardship, and suffering in Israel, at the time of Jonah. Thus, Nineveh was the last nation where the Prophet would have loved to preach a message of salvation.

Jonah's heart's desire was to see that sinful city and its entire population fall under the hammer of God's judgment. He worried that any intervention could cause the Ninevites to repent and attract divine mercy and forgiveness.

That was the last thing Jonah wanted for Nineveh and her people. He hoped that they would all perish in their wickedness. So, he boarded a ship and headed the opposite direction. He chose to run away to Tarshish rather than go Nineveh.

This displeased the Lord, and he sent a great storm and a mighty tempest to trouble the boat. The journey was so rough that everyone in the boat feared for his life. But when it was confirmed that the problem was because of Jonah, they threw him into the raging sea.

But God prepared a big fish which swallowed him. And after three days in the belly of the fish, with nothing to eat or drink, Jonah was vomited on the shores of Nineveh. This time around, the journey, though very scary for him, was smooth.

The best way to enjoy a sweet relationship with God is to do so in perfect obedience. Any believer who runs from God's assignment will endanger his soul, like Jonah. But the wise will in obedience turn many to righteousness and save their own souls too.

When Jonah eventually took God's warning to the people of Nineveh, they all responded positively, in the fear of the Lord. The king believed the word of God through Jonah, and called for a public fasting, with repentance.

Everyone and anything that had breath were involved in this total abstinence from food and water. They all wore sack clothes and sat in ashes. And after God saw the genuine repentance in their hearts, he forgave and gave them another chance.

Jonah came back to his right mind during the three days in the belly of the fish. He was forced to embark on a fast he did not plan for. No child of God should put himself through such risk or wait for a problem to arise before he can embark on a fast.

GROUP FASTING

Group fasting was a major part of worship in the Old Testament Bible. In fact, it was part of the requirements of the law for the religious feasts of Judaism. Every Jew was required by law to fast on all the feast days. The strangers in the land were also mandated to be part of this fast.

The kings of Israel often used this corporate method as an effective platform to seek the face of God during times of famine, and drought. And prophets as well as high priests also consecrated fasts as measures for repentance from the sins of the people.

TWENTY-ONE-DAY FAST.

Daniel and his three Hebrew friends, Hananiah, Misael and Azariah regularly engaged in fasts. At the beginning of their captivity, they jointly embarked on a ten-day partial fast. They ate nothing during this period save for vegetables and water.

And while still in captivity under king Darius who ruled over the Chaldeans, Daniel was provoked to embark on a fast following a disturbing vision he received. The bible did not state how long this fast lasted, but it records that he fasted and prayed until God answered him.

"In the first year of Darius the son of Ahasuerus, of the seed of the Medes, which was made king over the realm of the Chaldeans; 2 in the first year of his reign I Daniel understood by books the number of the years, whereof the word of the LORD came to Jeremiah the prophet, that he would accomplish seventy years in the desolations of Jerusalem. And I set my face unto the Lord God, to seek by prayer and supplications, with fasting, and sackcloth, and ashes:" (Daniel 9: 1-3).

Again, in the third year of Cyrus, king of Persia, Daniel engaged in a 21-days fast. The Bible specifically describes this program as a fruit and vegetable fast. He ate no pleasant bread and drank no wine during those days.

This fast he embarked on in Babylon became significant in biblical history for which every 21-days fast is now referred to as the Daniel fast. The twenty-one-day, Daniel's fast, is still popular among believers of this generation. (Daniel 1: 11-12, 15; 10 1-2).

PRAYER POINTS

1. My fasting and prayers shall attract attention, in Jesus' name.

2. My fasting and prayers shall result in angelic visitation, in Jesus' name.

3. Man of war, reveal battle strategies to me as I fast and pray, in Jesus' name.

4. My father, as I fast and pray, let my heavens open, in Jesus' name.

5. My fasting and prayers, cause confusion in the camp of my enemies, in Jesus' name.

6. My adversaries, receive the judgement of God, as I fast and pray, in Jesus' name.

7. My fasting and prayers shall bring my case before God, in Jesus' name.

8. Holy Spirit, open my senses to visions and revelations as I fast and pray, in Jesus' name.

9. My father, as I fast and pray, speak to me in my dreams, in Jesus' name.

10. Holy Spirit, lift my soul into the realm of the spirit as I fast and pray, in Jesus' name.

11. O God, separate me from friendships that will not improve my life, in Jesus' name.

12. O Lord, deliver my soul from the grip of vagabond spirits, in Jesus' name.

13. I arrest every spirit of bewitchment as I fast and pray, in Jesus' name.

14. Wandering spirits attacking my fasting and prayer, perish, in Jesus' name.

CHAPTER THREE

SOME BIBLE CHARACTERS THAT FASTED

MAN IS AN EXPRESSION OF GOD, WHOM HE FORMED IN HIS image and likeness with a mandate to manage his earthly kingdom. For a venture of this nature to profit the man, it is expected that the creature must obey the terms of his creator.

This calls for a complete adherence to God's rules which attract blessings of obedience and incur serious retributions to those who transgress the laws. But while worship revolves around faith, the fear of God, obedience to his word, and selfless sacrifice, are also important.

And while these factors, including humility and holiness are vital assets in worship, selfless sacrifice seem to predominate them all. This makes us to understand how God appreciates the sacrifice his children make in his honor.

This sacrificial model was originally established by God when he gave his only begotten Son to die for perishing human souls. He did this to reconcile humanity with himself through the blood of his son. Thus, God through Christ Jesus, made peace with the world of believers.

Before Jesus' crucifixion on the cross, no blood sacrifice met the divine interpretation of redemption. But with his death, resurrection, and ascension to his Father in heaven, all precious things offered to God in worship became acceptable symbols of true worship.

In the sphere of divine dominion therefore, a sacrifice includes the deliberate surrender of a man's total well-being for the benefit of others. This demands the extension of costly kindness which include the giving of things of irretrievable value, in the service of God and mankind.

So, to function effectively in the earthly kingdom, the carnal man must willingly, readily, and regularly engage in the surrender of his notable life, as a genuine offering on the altar of God. Selflessly relinquishing one's own interest for the sake of others delights God's heart.

Expressing God's nature in this manner allows for a true worship in spirit and in truth that attracts his attention. Without it, no one can enjoy a meaningful relationship with God or have valuable fellowship with him. Fasting is one special way of building this lasting relationship.

Honestly, no one fasts without a cause. There is often a dire need behind the urge to fast. And the Christian who promptly responds to this demand will reap its benefits because the rewards for this sacred solitude and sacrifice come with spiritual power.

Unfortunately, while the need for religious fasts will always exist, only few persons embrace it as a regular protocol, even with all its dues and benefits. So, this chapter will look at the positive impacts of fasting and prayer on the lives and ministries of those who embraced it.

There is no doubt that technology has transformed the earth into a rowdy society with all the noise regularly generated by about seven and half, billion souls. This has popularized the use of headphones, ear buds, and air-pods, among those with weak audio endurance capacity.

This self-inflicted problem has made it difficult for people to hear one another clearly. Added to this tumult is the uproar from trains, automobiles, airplanes, construction machinery, and other manufacturing equipment.

With all these noisy distractions, it is only certain that no one can clearly hear the voice of God even if he shouted from heaven. Loud and confused noise are weapons of the enemy against the human soul. Noise does not give the mind the calmness it needs to concentrate on God.

The Devil likes chaotic situations because it enables him to operate freely. Noise breeds confusion and enables demonic operations to thrive. But a religious fast will provide that peace and quietness required to hear the voice of God.

The early fathers of the faith realized the spiritual value of solitary times with God. They understood its benefits and exploited them. And given the crazier, louder, and more wicked society, believers in this generation need to do more to fraternize with God.

It is understandable that not everyone can engage in lengthy fasts like those notable characters in the Old Testament age and the early New Testament era. But endeavoring to fast will help any serious Christian to build and sustain a rewarding relationship with God.

It is helpful for igniting spiritual revival, to hear from God concerning a ministerial call, or to find clear direction in marriage, education, or in one's career. It is also useful for finding clarity about dreams, visions, revelations or for getting instructions in a situation.

"Then Daniel went to his house, and made the thing known to Hananiah, Mishael, and Azariah, his companions: That they would desire mercies of the God of heaven concerning this secret; that Daniel and his fellows should not perish with the rest of the wise men of Babylon. Then was the secret revealed unto Daniel in a night vision. Then Daniel blessed the God of heaven"(Daniel 2: 17-19)

"And he gave unto Moses, when he had made an end of communing with him upon mount Sinai, two tables of testimony, tables of stone, written with the finger of God" (Exodus 31: 18).

A few people in the Bible era appreciated the secret of fasting and maximized its power. They understood that it was one of the major keys to engaging God's attention, connecting to the provisions of his covenant, reasoning with him, and appropriating his blessings.

Every serious Christian needs the time to get away from the noise of society, and find a good place and valuable time, to listen to the voice of God. It was in such a solitary moment, that Elijah heard God's gentle voice as it clearly ministered to his spirit in a whisper.

Those who want to hear from the Holy Spirit must create time for this seclusion. He is a gentle Spirit and does not always manifest through great and strong winds, an earthquake, or in a fire. He also communicates through a gentle whisper.

"And he said, Go forth, and stand upon the mount before the LORD. And, behold, the LORD passed by, and a great and strong wind rent the mountains, and brake in pieces the rocks before the LORD; but the LORD was not in the wind: and after the wind an earthquake; but the LORD was not in the earthquake: And after the earthquake a fire; but the LORD was not in the fire: and after the fire a still small voice. And it was so, when Elijah heard it, that he wrapped his face in his mantle, and went out, and stood in the entering in of the cave. And, behold, there came a voice unto him, and said, What doest thou here, Elijah?" (1 Kings 19:11-13).

In the ancient past, God used people who gave their time to seek his face to execute his purpose for humanity. He is the same God and has not changed. And if God responded to their spiritual cries then, he will answer anyone now who will seek his face through fasting and prayer.

There is no doubt that some believers are genuinely interested in fasting. But they wait until it is inevitable. In the ancient Bible era, some people fasted and prayed as a matter of priority, and God blessed them in unusual ways. He does not forsake those who genuinely fast and pray.

Some of them include:

MOSES.

For anyone who has tried the mountain-top prayer and fasting, you know how difficult it is to haul food and drinks along. Mountain climbers will tell you that any added items on their bodies become load at certain heights as they go up.

In Moses' entire relationship with God, he went up to Mount Sinai on, at least, seven recorded occasions alone, to meet with God. On those trips, he did not take any baskets of bread or flasks of water. He denied himself all these that he might get word from God for his people.

(Exodus 19: 2-7, 8-11, 16, 20-25; 20: 1-17, 21; 23: 20-33).

Those visits to the top of Mt. Sinai often lasted some days. Moses spent three to seven days on some trips, but on three occasions he spent forty days. The only time they ate on the mountain was when he went along with Aaron, and seventy elders of Israel (Exodus 24: 10-13).

In the Bible, Moses tells the story himself, how he fasted for forty days and forty nights on that Mount Sinai before he received the Ten Commandments from God. These were the terms of the covenant which God wrote on the stone tablets with his fingers (Exodus 34:8).

But no sooner had Moses and Joshua gone up to Mount Sinai, than the people in the camp turned to worshipping a golden calf. This was an image of a heathen idol, which Aaron fashioned from the gold that all the Israelites in the camp contributed.

"And when the people saw that Moses delayed to come down out of the mount, the people gathered themselves together unto Aaron, and said unto him, Up, make us gods, which shall go before us; for as for this Moses, the man that brought us up out of the land of Egypt, we wot not what is become of him. And Aaron said unto them, Break off the golden earrings, which are in the ears of your wives, of your sons, and of your daughters, and bring them unto me. And all the people brake off the

golden earrings which were in their ears, and brought them unto Aaron. And he received them at their hand, and fashioned it with a graving tool, after he had made it a molten calf: and they said, These be thy gods, O Israel, which brought thee up out of the land of Egypt. And when Aaron saw it, he built an altar before it; and Aaron made proclamation, and said, Tomorrow is a feast to the LORD. *And they rose up early on the morrow, and offered burnt offerings, and brought peace offerings; and the people sat down to eat and to drink, and rose up to play. (Exodus 32: 1-6).*

The children of Israel had just come out of Egypt whose deities, "Hapi" and "Hathor", were linked with perverted sex. These idols were thought to control the power of fertility in both man and the land. Hapi, was also believed to be the intermediary between humans and gods.

The representations of these Egyptian gods were a bull and a heifer. The bull was the same symbol as Baal, another idol worshipped in Canaan, also believed to control fertility in that place. It was thus natural, though foolish, for the Israelites to seek after these idols.

They could not understand why Moses would abandon them for forty days and forty nights to bring them commandments from "a god" they could not see or touch. So, they suggested that Aaron make a golden calf.

But as Moses returned and heard the cry of their evil jubilation and sighted the shameful reason for their frenzied celebration, he smashed the two tablets of stone in his hands to pieces in anger. The people that God delivered for himself, had so soon chosen a substitute god for themselves.

"And it came to pass, as soon as he came nigh unto the camp, that he saw the calf, and the dancing: and Moses' anger waxed hot, and he cast the tables out of his hands, and brake them beneath the mount." (Exodus 32: 19)

"So I turned and came down from the mount, and the mount burned with fire: and the two tables of the covenant were in my two hands. And I looked, and, behold, ye had sinned against the LORD your God, and had made you a molten calf: ye had turned aside quickly out of the way which the LORD had commanded you. And I took the two tables, and cast them out of my two hands, and brake them before your eyes. And I fell down before the LORD, as at the first, forty days and forty nights: I did neither eat bread, nor drink water, because of all your sins which ye sinned, in doing wickedly in the sight of the LORD, to provoke him to anger" (Deuteronomy 9:15-18).

After this incident, Moses returned to Mount Sinai at the invitation of God for a replacement of commandments which he broke in anger before his brethren. And this time again, he had to embark on another program of a forty-day fasting and prayer.

QUEEN ESTHER (HADASA)

The historic book of Esther in the Old Testament captures a lot of drama, power-play, romance, and royal intrigues. But in the middle of this narrative is woven a sacred fast that played a key role in saving the lives of the Jews who lived in Persia under King Ahasuerus, at that time.

This Ahasuerus was the King who sat on the throne in Shushan and reigned in the kingdom of Persia which extended from India to Ethiopia. His territory covered a hundred and seven and twenty provinces overseen by princes, nobles, and servants. His wife's name was queen Vashti.

In the third year of his rule, he celebrated a lengthy feast to show off the wealth of his kingdom. And while his heart was merry with wine, he ordered the queen to parade before his guests and show her beauty. But the queen refused to do so and was banished from the throne for intransigence.

Later, and on the advice of the king's servants, all the fair, young virgins in the Empire were assembled in Shushan for a beauty pageant to replace Vashti. Among them was a Jewish orphan, Hadassah, who emerged as the King's choice from the contest. She was also known as Esther.

Meanwhile, Mordecai, another Jew, had become a palace official in the royal court. And from this privileged position, he helped expose a plot to assassinate King Ahasuerus. Incidentally, he was Hadassah's elder cousin who raised her after the death of her parents.

There was also in that royal court a man named Haman. He was the son of Hammedatha, an Amalekite. Haman was highly revered in the palace as one of the king's high officials that ruled over the princes in Persia. But he had a bitter hatred for the Jews.

And even while he enjoyed much power in the royal court, he still felt dishonored that Mordecai would not bow before him. Mordecai's strong religious belief as a

Jew forbade him from bowing before men and idols. So, Haman hated him the more (Genesis 23: 7)

Enraged by Mordecai's refusal to courtesy in his presence, he plots to annihilate all the Jews in the kingdom of Ahasuerus. With money paid and letters dispatched to all the regions of the royal kingdom, with the consent of the king, a date was set for the pogrom to begin.

At this critical point, Mordecai the Jew and cousin of Queen Esther reached out to her, if perhaps she could ask for the King's favor. Initially, Queen Esther was reluctant to go to the king. No one goes to the king except he or she was invited by him.

Esther was fully aware of the repercussion of breaking such royal protocol. But she also knew that the risk of remaining silent exposed her people to the great danger of death. Moreover, she was reminded by Mordecai that "she may have come to the palace for such a time as this".

So, she called for a fast. And the objective of it was to find favor before the king. No one could see the king without prior invitation. The consequence was death, but Queen Esther was determined to give her life for the sake of her people.

She had seen copies of the decree sent out by Haman to destroy the Jews and knew that her people will be exterminated if she did not act. So, she asked Mordecai to gather all the Jews in Shushan for a three-day, dry fast before she could go to the King. And she said, "if I perish, I perish".

"Then Esther bade them return Mordecai this answer, Go, gather together all the Jews that are present in Shushan,

and fast ye for me, and neither eat nor drink three days, night or day: I also and my maidens will fast likewise; and so will I go in unto the king, which is not according to the law: and if I perish, I perish" (Esther 4: 15-16).

The queen fasted and encouraged the people to fast along with her. The threat by Haman bolstered her into action. She became passionate to save the lives of her people by selflessly giving her own life mindful that her decision could lead to her own death.

She was strengthened during the fast and she received the boldness to go to the king. To the glory of God, the three-day fasting yielded a favorable result. The Queen's fast did not end in vain because it resulted in a great deliverance.

The King not only gave audience to queen Esther as she requested but granted her all her heart's desires. And in addition, Mordecai the Jew was rewarded with honor for saving the king's life from an insurrection and he became an esteemed official in the royal palace.

The King also permitted Queen Esther, contrary to the laws of the Medes and Persians, to reverse the death letter written by Haman against the Jews. Instead, the Jews in all the kingdom of Ahasuerus were given the permission to lay hands on those that sought after their lives.

At last, the queen saved the Jews from the plot of extermination. Haman the enemy of the Jews was hanged on the gallows he prepared to hang Mordecai, and the Jews received royal permission to destroy those who had planned to kill them.

Although the Book of Esther is one of the two books of the Bible where "God" is not mentioned (the other is the

Songs of Solomon), yet we find the fingerprints of God in all the chapters. From the beginning of the book, we see God exposing the enemies of his children.

Quickly, following suit, God is seen working behind the scenes to unseat Queen Vashti causing the nobles to arrange a beauty pageant that involved an unknown Jewish girl. All these were part of God's agenda to forestall the genocide planned against the Jews.

Also, Queen Esther's fast had an objective. And it was to find favor before the king. Only the Al-knowing, All-seeing, Wise God, who has the heart of the kings in his hand could have given her all her heart's desire. And she got all she desired because she fasted to a living God.

KING DAVID.

The Bible describes David as the greatest king of Israel. He is even so highly revered that the scriptures testify of him, in God's own words, as "a man after God's heart". Even Jesus the Messiah is referred to in the Bible as the "Son of David".

But Bible history records his adulterous sin with Bathsheba, the wife of Uriah, the Hittite. After it, David learns that Bathsheba was pregnant with a child and asks Joab his commander to position Uriah at the deadliest part of the battle. That was where Uriah was killed.

Thereafter, David took Uriah's widow to be his wife. She had the child and David loved him. But it was not long before David's secret was exposed by Nathan the prophet. David accepted responsibility for the sin, confessed, and repented of it. But soon, the child became extremely sick.

At this point, David began to fast and pray hoping that God would save the boy's life contrary to the word of the prophet. He neither ate nor drank anything while the child was ill. But the child died on the seventh day. Thereafter, David broke his fast.

God created man in his image and likeness and endowed him with a godly heart full of selfless love, and compassion for others. So, from Abraham through Joseph to Moses, he waited to find that person after his heart to show up.

When he found these virtues in David, he did not hesitate to anoint him King over his people. Though David was not a perfect being, yet God used him because he had a rare virtue and readiness to sacrifice his life for God's cause and for his people.

David's imperfection, however, led him to commit adultery. This was a sad turning point in his relationship with God. And God made him pay for his transgression. David immediately embarks on a fast to ask for forgiveness and for the life of the boy.

When a man's actions are aligned with God, his sacrifice can make way for him before God. But the prayer of an unrighteous person is abomination before God. This was the situation David found himself in the matter of Bathsheba, and he paid the price.

So, despite abstaining from food and drinks for seven days, laying on the ground and refraining from anointing himself and washing, God denied David his desire. He forgave him alright, but the child did not survive. (2 Samuel 12: 15-20).

PROPHET ELIJAH

Prophet Elijah also fasted and for a lengthy period too. After he had killed the prophets of Baal and Asherah he received a death threat from Jezebel. So, he ran to Beersheba, left his servant there and went a day's journey further into the wilderness to mourn and grieve his soul.

He prayed that God would take his life. But God had other plans. God wanted him to consecrate his replacement before he would call him home. So, he fed him with just enough food that enabled him to travel over 200 miles in forty days.

People fast for several reasons. In this case, Elijah was depressed and fearful. He was so scared that he ran into hiding. In situations like this, people turn to fasting to regain their faith, sanity, and boldness. So, Elijah continued to fast until an angel rescued him with cake and water.

This was the last food and water that Elijah tasted. And he went in the strength of that food for forty days. Only a few people can fast this long without food or water. That is why the Devil has used the avenue of the human appetite to ruin many Christian destinies.

JEHOSHAPHAT.

Ancient biblical literature shows that fasting was a permanent feature of Judaism. Then, individual fasts were based on personal needs. But the prerogative to call for a group fast as required by Torah rested on the elders or at the request of the king. (1 Kings 21: 8-12).

Jehoshaphat was king of Judah at a difficult time in the nation's history. But, unlike his predecessors, he was a King that feared God. So, when a vast army of adversaries came against him, he set his face to seek the Lord. And he did this by proclaiming a fast throughout all Judah.

*"**Some people came and told Jehoshaphat, "A vast army is coming against you from Edom,**[a] **from the other side of the Dead Sea. It is already in Hazezon Tamar" (that is, En Gedi). Alarmed, Jehoshaphat resolved to inquire of the LORD, and he proclaimed a fast for all Judah" (2 Chronicles 20: 2—3)(NIV)).***

Jehoshaphat's method was an uncommon strategy. He chose to report the matter to God through a national fast. He understood that the battle was beyond the power of carnal weapons. So, he turned to God by employing the weapon of a fast.

Every child of God must understand that the spiritual realm is the territory for warfare. It is the best place to defeat the enemy for those who know their way. The King of Judah understood this clearly and took the battle to the heavenlies where he discomfited his enemies.

When you invite God into your battle through a fast, the size of your army will no longer count. Thus, Jehoshaphat's small army scored a great victory against a multitude and returned with abundant riches and precious jewels. (2 Chronicles 20: 25).

PROPHET JEREMIAH.

Fasting pleases God, more so, when it is embarked on to seek his face. Many serious servants of God understood this secret and Jeremiah was one of them. So, he took part in all the post exilic fasts and those in remembrance of the events that led to the destruction of the Temple.

In the ancient days of Judaism, a fast could be prompted by many reasons. Apart from the days specified in the Torah, the nation fasted on the death of a national leader, in response to repentance from sin, as way of averting calamity, in times of emergencies, or before going to war.

Prophet Jeremiah, also known as the weeping prophet, engaged in all these fasts. And even when he was confined (for crying out against the sins of the people and the king) and was unable to go into the temple, he still took part in the emergency fast (Jeremiah 36:9).

KING DARIUS.

Many other people in the Bible fasted, both in the Old and New Testaments. Even Darius, the gentile king and friend of Daniel who was deceived to throw him into the den of lions fasted. Daniel had envious enemies in the kingdom.

They did not like him because he occupied a higher position above all the princes. They knew he prayed three times a day to his God and plotted against him. So, they got the king to proclaim an edict preventing anyone from praying to any other deity or power except to the king.

They knew how much Daniel loved to pray to his God and that only such a decree could pitch him against the king. So, after the decree was signed, they caught Daniel praying and threw him into the den of lions, according to the decree of the king.

That night, the bible says that the king could not sleep. He allowed no music to be played and he gave up all food and his normal pleasures. And before daybreak the king ran to the den of lions to find out what had become of Daniel.

When he discovered that Daniel was still alive, he was exceedingly glad and commanded that the men who conspired against Daniel be cast into the den of lions. He then made a proclamation that everyone in his kingdom worship the God of Daniel (Daniel 6: 18-28)

OUR LORD JESUS CHRIST.

Our Lord Jesus Christ was one of the great Bible characters that lived a fasted life. His longest fast was the one preceding the onset of his ministry. During that time, he spent forty days and forty nights without food in the wilderness, while the Devil tempted him (Matthew 4:1-8).

His daily life thereafter was entirely consumed with teaching the public, preaching the gospel, and ministering healing and deliverance, that he scarcely had time to eat. His life and ministry focused mainly on saving perishing souls.

And even though he ate natural food, like all humans, it was not a priority to him as he did not spend much time feasting on physical foods and drinks. This explains why he said, "My food is to do the will of Him who sent me". (John 4: 34).

Thus, by regularly abstaining from natural foods, Jesus taught his disciples the power of selfless sacrifice. He taught them to pray also. But beyond that, he explained the right attitude of a fast, and revealed its benefits to them.

"Moreover when ye fast, be not, as the hypocrites, of a sad countenance: for they disfigure their faces, that they may appear unto men to fast. Verily I say unto you, They have their reward. But thou, when thou fastest, anoint thine head, and wash thy face; That thou appear not unto men to fast, but unto thy Father which is in secret: and thy Father, which seeth in secret, shall reward thee openly.(Matthew 6: 16-18).

That the disciples continued to routinely fast even after Jesus' ascension to heaven was proof that they understood how important and inevitable it was in Christian life and ministry. It was Jesus' secret weapon for subduing tough problems and his disciples embraced it.

APOSTLE PAUL.

Saul was born in Tarsus. But as a Pharisee zealous for God, and raised according to the perfect law of Judaism, it is certain that he fasted regularly. This practice was not new to him. No wonder it was his first religious act following his conversion.

Saul was on his way to Damascus to arrest disciples of Jesus and bring them bound to the high Priest in Jerusalem for judgment. Many disciples had already fled Jerusalem for fear of persecution following the stoning to death of Stephen by an angry religious mob.

But on the way, Saul lost his sight after he encountered lightening from heaven. He was led into Damascus as a blind man by his companions who heard the same voice as Saul but confessed that they saw no one. In the three days that followed, Saul ate no food (Acts 9: 9).

After that experience, Saul now Paul, became an ambassador of the gospel of Christ that he once persecuted, living the rest of his life in fasts, shipwrecks, and jails. In his second epistle to the church at Corinth, the apostle said that these were the price he paid for Christ (2 Corinthians 11: 25-30).

Regular sacrifice of food and water became a standard practice in his life to the extent that he once fasted for fourteen days. This bolstered his faith in his new relationship with Christ. It also enabled him to see the power of the Holy Spirit in other people and in his own life.

"As they ministered to the Lord, and fasted, the Holy Ghost said, Separate me Barnabas and Saul for the work whereunto I have called them. And when they had fasted and prayed, and laid their hands on them, they sent them away." (Acts 13: 2-3)

"And while the day was coming on, Paul besought them all to take meat, saying, This day is the fourteenth day that ye have tarried and continued fasting, having taken nothing." (Acts 27: 33).

Apart from the few Bible characters mentioned above, there were others in the Old and New Testament whose fasts were exceptional. They include people like prophet Ezekiel, apostles Peter, Barnabas, James, John, and many female disciples of Jesus.

Ruth was a Moabitess who followed Naomi's God and ended up in the genealogy of Jesus. She would also have fasted according to the Law. Latter Gentile converts like Cornelius, the Roman Centurion, and many unnamed disciples of Jesus are on record to have fasted like their master.

PRAYER POINTS

1. Holy Spirit, create in me the hunger for spiritual growth, in Jesus' name.

2. O Lord, let me find forgiveness, grace and mercy, in Jesus' name.

3. Holy Spirit, revive my spirit and ignite my fasting and prayer altar with your fire, in Jesus' name.

4. Holy Ghost fire, cleanse my soul as I fast and pray, in Jesus' name.

5. O Lord, strengthen my spirit in the inner man to overcome temptation, in Jesus' name.

6. Word of God, weaken my flesh and strengthen my spirit, in Jesus' name.

7. Holy Spirit, baptize me with Spiritual gifts for ministry, in Jesus' name.

8. O God, help me to overcome the lusts of the flesh, in Jesus' name.

9. Holy Spirit, enable my mind to always focus on spiritual things, in Jesus' name.

10. My prayer and fasting shall not be in vain, in Jesus' name.

11. Bread of life, make my spirit, soul, and body to be in good health, in Jesus' name.

12. No weapon fashioned against my spirit, soul, or body shall prosper, in Jesus' name.

13. God of all flesh, hear and answer me, in Jesus' name.

14. Holy Spirit, help me to fast and pray according to God's will, in Jesus' name.

CHAPTER FOUR

SHOULD A CHRISTIAN FAST?

Man lives in a sinful world.

SINCE THE FALL OF ADAM AND EVE IN THE GARDEN OF Eden, mankind has lived in a sin polluted world ruled by Satan. And due to the corruption in this world system it has been easy for this enemy of mankind to further seduce the human soul to keep the man under bondage.

And Satan has masterfully accomplished this agenda by preying on the human soul by giving him gifts that his flesh finds difficult to reject. This way, he continued to violate the human spirit, and ravage his flesh, in readiness to destroy his soul in hell (John 10:10).

Man was created by God to be a revealer of his semblance on earth. And there is a similitude of God's characters in any man who's will is controlled by the will of God. This leads to peace in the kingdom of God.

To retain this peace and enjoy all of God's benefits on earth, man was required to live up to the divine codes of righteousness. By obeying God's laws, he would maintain order on earth and be in harmony with God. The Devil did not want this accord. So, he battled against it.

If he did not fight this growth, the soul of every person born anew in Christ will find it easy to stay in tune with the will of God. This kind of relationship will enable the natural man easy access to the riches of God in heaven from the earth.

That kind of rapport between man and his God would not be in the interest of this man of perdition. Peace does not favor his operations. So, wherever there is order, he throws his hammer into the works to bring confusion.

With the carnal man, it was easy to twist God's word and use it out of context to deceive his soul. Thus, he made Adam and Eve to disobey God and fall out of favor with Him. Taking scriptures out of context is the Devil's area of specialization.

Satan prevailed against the first Adam because he was naïve and unprepared against his tricks. But he failed at his attempt with Jesus because Jesus was ready, having fasted and prayed. So, he overcame the evil one (Genesis 3: 1-7; Matthew 4: 5-7).

It benefits the Devil when a soul is unable to resist his tactics. So, he likes to go after souls and discourage them from fasting and praying. Especially as these disciplines prepare the believer in establishing sweet fellowship and enjoying affectionate friendship with God.

Unfortunately, Christians who will not fast and pray the way they should, will fall for the Devil's tricks, grieve the Holy Spirit, and will not manifest the gifts of God. But a Believer whose mind is controlled by God's Spirit will be Christlike and be an extraordinary friend of God.

To be an extraordinary friend of God, a person must be ready to do extraordinary things for him. To stand out for God requires doing some outstanding acts. That is why all the extraordinary characters in the Bible were people who did extraordinary things.

A fast is a believer's evidence of total submission, and the desire to be possessed by God. For the Christian, it makes room for the infilling by the Holy Spirit, which enables the operation of God's gifts through such a child of God

From Abraham, who quit his father's house, his people, their gods, and altars of his ancestors, to Joseph who fled from the inner chambers of a philandering, Egyptian housewife, all were people of impeachable characters in whose hearts was the desire to be possessed God.

The common denominator in their lives was their total faith in God and their readiness to sacrifice their lives for him. This was what inspired the three young Hebrew slaves in Babylon to opt to be cast into a seven-fold heated furnace, rather than bow to Nebuchadnezzar's idol.

It is easy to be faithful when all is well and there are no challenges in the Christian's life. But true loyalty is known when the storms of life arise because the untested believer is vulnerable to the whiles of the enemy. Fasting will help a Christian to be ready for this season.

In the Old Testament, God gave his Law to the children of Israel through Moses. And this law included a command to fast on the Day of Atonement. (Leviticus 16: 29). The New Testament Christian is not under any such law. For him, fasting is a personal decision.

But because Jesus fasted before the beginning of his ministry and continued to do so thereafter, he set a model which his disciples adopted. So, Christians now follow this pattern with the understanding that if Jesus did it, then it must be good, profitable, and beneficial.

A Christian who does not fast will easily be blinded by the god of this age. This will make him incapable of seeing the light of the gospel of Christ who is the image of God and so become vulnerable to the Devil. Such a Christian be easy prey of the wicked and captive of the mighty.

It is a tragedy to find Christians who get scared when the Devil sneezes. But this is the ugly condition of many Bible-believers because they scarcely find time to strengthen their spirits, souls, and bodies for the inevitable spiritual battles of life.

"And the very God of peace sanctify you wholly; and I pray God your whole spirit and soul and body be preserved blameless unto the coming of our Lord Jesus Christ" (1 Thessalonians 5: 23)

The human body constitutes the spirit, the soul, and the flesh. The spirit is the innermost part of his being and the part that connects with the spirit realm. By its nature, it is invisible and can perceive vibrations from the portal of the spirit realm through dreams, visions, and revelations.

The spirit of a man is the organ for hearing what is spoken in the realm of the spirits, whether good or bad. It is also the alarm system that warns the soul of things that are righteous or evil because it is conscious of spiritual things.

The soul represents a man's invisible personality. It is the engine-room of his emotions and the seat of his feelings, affections, hurts, love, and hate. It is the place where human imaginations, thoughts, and will are conceived. It is also the control button of good or evil actions.

Therefore, the soul needs to be continually nurtured by the word of God or it will be captured by the Devil and polluted by evil. Natural food can sustain the flesh, while silver and gold may decorate it. But only the word of God can preserve the soul.

Thus, human life is only meaningful when the mind is nourished by God's word. A soul that is not well nourished with God's word will not survive in the day of affliction. That life will perish because it was not prepared to deal with the realities of life.

The flesh is the third component of the entire being. It is that part of the body that is in direct contact with the fallen world. In its reprobate state, it desires to gratify all lusts. But this is not good for the soul and the spirit which are eternal in nature.

It is made up of three parts. These include the skin (the outer covering), the bones that support the body, and the blood that transports nutrients, oxygen, and removes carbon dioxide and poisons via essential organs.

From the natural arrangement by God, the spirit is created to rule over the soul and the flesh. When a man's spirit loses this natural position to the soul, emotional problems begin to manifest in its body because the flesh is always at war with the soul. (Romans 8: 5-13)

Everyone is responsible for the condition of his spirit, soul, and body. A man's whole being is referred to as the temple of the Holy Spirit. And as the only creature that has a spirit, each man is accountable for his spirit, his soul, and his body.

Generally, people do not pay enough attention to their spirits the way they do to their natural bodies. The normal practice is to nourish the flesh, which will perish someday, while neglecting the soul and spirit that will live forever. Fasting will help a Christian to reverse this pattern.

The soul of a man and his spirit are virtually linked together even though they have different functions and can influence the other. But a man's whole being benefits more from God when his spirit is in control. A person that is ruled by the spirit becomes a spiritual super-power.

At the soul level, man does not have much control of his actions. And when the soul is in control, as is the case in the reprobate life, that individual is just like a human robot subject to demonic manipulations and material lusts.

God's original divine arrangement for mankind was not for the human soul to control his spirit. Only unregenerated beings live this way. And whenever this is the case, that life turns out rebellious. This explains why an unrighteous man cannot obey God.

But after the new birth, the Holy Spirit takes over the control of the spirit. This is how God designed it to be. And as that Christian grows in grace, it becomes easier for his spirit to connect with the spirit of God and obey his will.

From the moment the human spirit takes control of the soul, the body can be trained to obey God's righteous demands. It becomes easy to influence the soul, discipline the flesh and bring them under control as the spirit would not permit them to run amock.

A revived spirit is the reward of focusing on God. The spirit that is in deep communion with God will not succumb to transgression. In this condition, it is difficult for that life to fall for any seduction or be fooled by any temptation from the Devil.

Any believer that is seeking the face of God by abstaining from the material pursuits and worldly cares will attract divine attention. He will not only embrace the joy of the Holy Ghost but will be rewarded with the knowledge of the secrets of God.

In the stillness and surrender occasioned by a fast, the human spirit can bring his flesh under control. Such subjection will help the mind to concentrate on God and the person of Christ, thereby rebuffing all satanic distractions.

The result is a great transformation in ways that make the whole being more sensitive to the feelings of God. That is when the soul begins to hate what God hates, and the mind starts to think like God does, and the body becomes hungry to do what God desires.

God is concerned with what a Christian does with his entire body. As the temple of the Holy Spirit, the flesh should not be involved with ungodly things. A redeemed spirit must be able to positively influence the desires of its flesh. Fasting will help a Christian achieve this result.

"Neither yield ye your members as instruments of unrighteousness unto sin: but yield yourselves unto God,

as those that are alive from the dead, and your members as instruments of righteousness unto God" (Romans 6: 13).

"What? know ye not that your body is the temple of the Holy Ghost which is in you, which ye have of God, and ye are not your own? For ye are bought with a price: therefore glorify God in your body, and in your spirit, which are God's" (1 Corinthians 6: 19-20).

It is certain that any human soul that is spiritually famished will be weak and vulnerable to the Devil. That is why a Christian must form the habit of fasting. Fasting provides a Christian the ample opportunity to feed on solid spiritual food.

"Baby-Christians" depend mainly on "spiritual milk". No committed Christian will settle for a diet that will not help him develop strong spiritual muscles. Only a well-planned and properly executed fast will create the right time for this kind of sacrifice.

The result is uncommon spiritual growth that equips the believer with the right tools to face the Devil when he turns up with the inevitable problems of life. The baby-steps of a believer on spiritual milk cannot do this work.

But the Christian fast must not stop with caring only for the spirit and the soul. Rather, it should also extend to caring for the entire body by being mindful of what is fed to the flesh through the eyes, the ears, and the mouth (Romans 10: 17).

Most teachings on fasting focus on its benefits to the spirit and the soul, forgetting the flesh. This idea misses the fact that whatever affects one part of the entire being undoubtedly affects the rest. As a result, it is only wise to consider the effects of a fast on the human flesh.

Another reason a Christian should fast is because it helps to put to death all the immoral junk and carnal ideas his flesh consumes via the natural senses. What a believer feeds his flesh will influence his soul. So, no part of the body should be exposed to the wrong thing.

Thus, when a Christian abstains from regular foods and pleasures, to feed his spirit-man with God's word, his mind is tuned to perceiving things from God's perspective. This process helps in the transformation of a man's entire body as a living sacrifice for God's use.

No one can get enough of God's word. Setting time aside to drink from the fountain of his word is the only way of keeping the mind wise, knowledgeable and in peace. Only one word from God can change a life for good.

"I beseech you therefore, brethren, by the mercies of God, that ye present your bodies a living sacrifice, holy, acceptable unto God, which is your reasonable service. And be not conformed to this world: but be ye transformed by the renewing of your mind, that ye may prove what is that good, and acceptable, and perfect, will of God" (Romans 12: 1-2).

Furthermore, the process of a religious fast helps a Christian to forge a closer relationship with God. The willful denial of daily nutrients and worldly pleasures to the body to seek God's friendship delights his heart. Drawing near to God in this manner has many gracious rewards.

God's promise is that he will draw near to those who draw near to him. Part of that promise is fulfilled when a Christian humbly submits to him expressing his need of forgiveness, asking for mercy, and declaring his insufficiency without God.

Through sacrificial worship, a Christian can successfully gain access into the presence of the almighty God. Uncommon access of this nature always attracts divine attention. And heaven always responds to the requests tabled before God on such occasions.

The world is too noisy and filled with distractions that make it difficult for many to enjoy meaningful quiet time with God. But a fast provides that ample opportunity to spend valuable time to refresh intimacy with a loving God.

It enables a Christian to disengage from all manner of bitterness, wrath, anger, lust, and evil speaking. No Christian that is fasting can at the same time keep malice and carry about a baggage of hurts, hate and unforgiveness.

So, a fast will help to take a Christian's mind away from the evil distortions in this world that pervert the soul. The carnal mind is always in pursuit of material things and other forms of godlessness that will not attract a righteous God.

During a fast, the natural man has extra time to dig deeper into the mysteries of God enshrined in his word. Such spiritual knowledge leads to great spiritual growth, power, and greater awe for God. These factors make a man to honor God as he desires and deserves.

That is why a Christian should fast regularly. Because it will help him focus on spiritual things so he can live in obedience to God's word. Obedience is evidence of the soul in love with God. Those who are in love with God are not likely to walk in the flesh.

Thus, by regularly fasting, a Christian's spirit, soul and body will be in tune with the spirit of God and do his will. This way, that Christian will receive power to deal with his emotions, and grace to experience the daily move of the Holy Spirit in his life.

"Submit yourselves therefore to God. Resist the devil, and he will flee from you. Draw nigh to God, and he will draw nigh to you. Cleanse your hands, ye sinners; and purify your hearts, ye double minded" (James 4: 7-8).

The desire of the carnal man is focused on satisfying the flesh. This carnal mindset motivated by sin perverts the soul. But fasting helps reverse this evil pattern by abstaining from carnal things that sustain the flesh and replacing them with spiritual things that nourish the soul.

Jesus regards all believers as his friends. And it is usual for friends to share secrets with one another. So, the interaction that ensues during a fast, results in the exchange of useful information. That is when God makes his will to be known to men.

It is true that every Christian is a child of God. But some children become special sons by maturing in intimacy with their father than the others. Their relationship is different, and they get to wear the coat of many colors for the common secrets they share.

People who have friends they trust tell them intimate secrets. God operates same way with his sons too. He trusted Moses so much he gave him the constitution for

Israel and revealed things to him that he could not share with other natural men.

In the Bible, God specifically described some people as his friends. As a result, he revealed secrets that were kept away from others to them. Jesus also called his disciples his friends. And in the same manner, he taught them the mysteries of God's kingdom.

"And the disciples came, and said unto him, Why speakest thou unto them in parables? He answered and said unto them, Because it is given unto you to know the mysteries of the kingdom of heaven, but to them it is not given. For whosoever hath, to him shall be given, and he shall have more abundance: but whosoever hath not, from him shall be taken away even that he hath. Therefore speak I to them in parables: because they seeing see not; and hearing they hear not, neither do they understand." (Matthew 13: 10-13).

The way God interacted with Abraham shows one of his methods in dealing with his faithful friends. He goes out of the normal path to connect with them and teach them his secrets before delegating special assignments to them.

So, through a fast, a Christian can establish friendship with God. The benefit of this is that such a Christian begins to get a clearer picture of the image and character of God. This will also place him where he can get a better understanding of the true nature of God.

In the pursuit for intimate friendship with God, many characters in the Bible made sacrifices that put God on a higher priority above any friendship with the world.

This explains why Moses pleased God with this selfless sacrifice.

In the same way, the Christian who commits to a god-approved, selfless denial will be compensated. To such friends of God, he reveals his ways, while to the rest, he just shows them his acts. This was God's level of intimacy with his friend Abraham and with Moses.

"And the LORD said, Shall I hide from Abraham that thing which I do; Seeing that Abraham shall surely become a great and mighty nation, and all the nations of the earth shall be blessed in him? For I know him, that he will command his children and his household after him, and they shall keep the way of the LORD, to do justice and judgment; that the LORD may bring upon Abraham that which he hath spoken of him." (Genesis 18: 17-19).

"He made known his ways unto Moses, his acts unto the children of Israel." (Psalm 103: 7).

Thus, a Christian should fast, to maintain the sacred standards that God demands for sustained relationship with him. This opens the curtain of heaven for God to clothe his chosen ones with strength to overcome the enemy and keep the Devil from making them victims.

The enemy knows when a child of God is weak. He knows all the areas of his human frailties and understands the right time to strike. He knows that a mind will lust after evil if it is continually exposed to sin. So, he will take advantage of his moments.

Fasting, like prayer, praise, faith, and obedience is an inevitable step through which a Christian can reach the place of victory. But there is always the chance that the Devil will hinder the Christian from taking this step that will fill him with power.

Thus, the Christian that is truly hungry and thirsty for the gifts and power of the Holy Ghost will make deliberate efforts to turn his back to the Devil. He must shut his ears and eyes to what the Devil is offering as it can never be better than what he will receive from God after a fast.

Fasting keeps man's relationship with God fresh and intact and makes a Christian to live his best life without the spiritual complications posed by fear, doubts, worries and anxieties. It is a way of embracing God to possess supernatural "fire" to operate in his anointing.

Fasting is a humbling experience in self-denial that results in the regeneration of the spirit and the soul. The result is a brand-new life that is weaned of the appetites and nostalgia for staple lusts that diminish the virtues of Christ in the human nature (Philippians 3:8).

A person who is humble before God will certainly to be exalted by him. God lifts the humble in spirit and appreciates every Christian who in thankfulness sets valuable time aside to worship him, and to recall all his goodness.

Fasting helps the soul to remain vigilant against the tricks of the Devil. It is a sign of utter reliance on God in the battle against evil and empowers a person to subdue pride which is the root of the sin of self-dependence. It helps a Christian to walk in humility instead of arrogance.

By fasting, a Christian reaffirms his unflinching confidence in the person and word of God. A Christian who utterly leans on God in the battles of life will be blessed with victories, but one who does not rely on him will fall before the Devil.

"Humble yourselves therefore under the mighty hand of God, that he may exalt you in due time:" (1 Peter 5: 6).

The spirit of a Christian who fasts regularly will receive protection from the domain of supernatural light. God is light and the glitter of his divine presence disperses all forms of evil darkness. And the radiance of his glory when seen in man causes the Devil to bow.

A Christian who fasts regularly will be established on a platform of spiritual resources. God is the all-sufficient provider and in the riches of his glory are an abundance of all good things which are the heritage of the children of God.

No believer can ever get enough of God. So, a Christian fast must be a deliberate attempt at satisfying an insatiable hunger for more of God and to express the conscious desire to have less or nothing of what the world offers (John 3:30).

So, a Christian should fast and express his spiritual destitution and the desire to correct the situation. This provides him the opportunity to surrender his weaknesses and be strengthened with the "bread of life". Otherwise, that Christian will continue to live in spiritual malnutrition.

The human soul becomes sick when there is lack, or not enough spiritual nourishment to sustain it. But as a Christian engages in regular communion with God through his word, it affects his spiritual life in a positive way leading to a blessed state of mind.

Fasting exposes the human heart to the light of God. As this light permeates the mind, it enlightens it making the knowledge of God's word more pleasant to the soul. This leads to a deeper understanding of God's laws and his judgements.

No one can ever have enough of God. But by spending meaningful time in his presence, anyone can receive the power to produce righteous fruit such as peace, joy, love, compassion, faith, and other virtues that will be useful in time of need.

These are some of the benefits a person can receive by staying in the presence of God. It will also guarantee the protection of the Holy Spirit and assure the human soul uncommon preservation. This creates room for effective fellowship with God.

Some schools of thought have argued that denying the body food is not a necessity when the believer can pray without going that far. Well, any Christian that appreciates what God gave up for the sake of humanity will abstain from food for a few days as a show of gratitude.

A person can pray anytime and anywhere. And even when some kinds of prayer, such as "quiet time with God", call for seclusion, effective fasting in our noisy world demands special isolation to keep away from any distractions.

"Being forty days tempted of the devil. And in those days he did eat nothing: and when they were ended, he afterward hungered." (Luke 4: 2).

Meaningful fasting helps in the preservation of the human body as an offering (living sacrifice) unto God. It is a radical departure from the usual prayer which does not require any prior schedule and does not call for any form of sacrifice.

Prayer is obviously a notable way of communicating with God. A fast however, is different. It requires adequate planning to be meaningful and effective because of the separation involved and the sacrifice that goes along with it.

"(For the LORD thy God is a merciful God;) he will not forsake thee, neither destroy thee, nor forget the covenant of thy fathers which he sware unto them." (Deuteronomy 4: 31).

"Let us therefore come boldly unto the throne of grace, that we may obtain mercy, and find grace to help in time of need." (Hebrews 4: 16)

It is the Christian's best shot at forgiveness, receiving God's grace, and reconciling with God. It is an extremely important time for staying away from the world of evil to recalibrate one's faith and remind oneself that God is still in control of his soul.

"And Jesus being full of the Holy Ghost returned from Jordan, and was led by the Spirit into the wilderness, Being forty days tempted of the devil. And in those days he did eat nothing: and when they were ended, he afterward hungered." (Luke 4: 1-2)

"He giveth power to the faint; and to them that have no might he increaseth strength." (Isaiah 40: 29)

Fasting changes things in the spirit realm. It assists a believer to access a higher dimension of spiritual experience. This brings great benefits to the soul without causing any mortal harm or injuries to the physical body.

The process of a religious fast helps a Christian to unclog his mind from the vicious debris of sexual lusts, pornography, deadly drug, and tobacco deposits. It keeps the mind from fantasizing on evil thoughts, and unfruitful imaginations that bring condemnation to the soul.

This type of life boosts a Christian's spiritual energy and increases the boldness. In this mode, his soul and the flesh come under the control of the spirit. And for a spirit that is linked with the spirit of God, nothing can go wrong.

Fasting will help a Christian to deal with desperate situations when they arise. Queen Esther's fast, along with all the Jews, during the reign of King Ahasuerus, is an inspiring example. God answered them when they turned to him in their desperation.

"Go, gather together all the Jews that are present in Shushan, and fast ye for me, and neither eat nor drink three days, night or day: I also and my maidens will fast likewise; and so will I go in unto the king, which is not according to the law: and if I perish, I perish. So, Mordecai went his way, and did according to all that Esther had commanded him." (Esther 4: 16-17).

Difficult situations require difficult actions. Fasting may be tough initially, but the body can concentrate more when food is taken out of the way. Too much eating and drinking take away the time a Christian can spend to worship God.

God did not disappoint Queen Esther. Instead, he swiftly came to her rescue. The decree issued by Haman to destroy the Jews was reversed, Haman's house was transferred to Mordecai and authority was handed to the Jews to avenge themselves on their enemies.

A fasted soul perseveres in the face life's battles and knows how to always lean on God. Such a Christian does not take God's favors for granted and relies on his mercy and graces for healing, deliverance, and restoration when in need.

The Christian who denies his body food and other comforts to spend time with God will certainly be rewarded with his love and an overflow of his kindness. In the end, his heart will be filled with gladness more than when his stomach was filled with corn and wine (Matthew 5:6).

Fasting helps a Christian to keep on the divine path. It motivates him to live for God and operate in the power of his divine knowledge, understanding and wisdom. It reinforces a Christian's faith and enables him to operate at a higher level of trust in God.

"Trust in the LORD with all thine heart; and lean not unto thine own understanding. In all thy ways acknowledge him, and he shall direct thy paths." (Proverbs 3: 5-6).

PRAYER POINTS

1. Every situation that has defied prayers in my life, receive solution as I fast now, in Jesus' name.

2. O God, let my fasting and prayer be like sweet incense before you, in Jesus' name.

3. Holy Spirit, strengthen me as I fast and pray, in Jesus' name.

4. O Lord, disgrace the powers assigned to disgrace me, in Jesus' name.

5. Let my fasting and prayer confuse my enemies, in Jesus' name.

6. Powers resorting to ancient records in search of reason to harm me, shall not prosper, in Jesus' name.

7. Son of Man, step into the fiery furnace and deliver me, in Jesus' name.

8. O Lord, by the power of your wonders, rescue me from every destruction, in Jesus' name.

9. Known and unknown sickness in my body be healed as I fast and pray, in Jesus' name.

10. Angel of God visit me in this fasting program, in Jesus' name.

11. O Lord, reverse the plan of every "Haman" over my life, in Jesus' name.

12. O God, save me from the hand of my oppressors, in Jesus' name.

13. My father, deliver me from darkness and every shadow of death, in Jesus' name.

14. Voice of the blood of Jesus, silence every storm in my life, in Jesus' name.

CHAPTER FIVE

JESUS' ATTITUDE TO FASTING

FASTING WAS A MANDATE IN THE OLD TESTAMENT. AND as a Jew, Jesus is on Bible record to have fasted, not only according to the law of Moses, but like Moses before he began his ministry. This was the forty days fast during which the Devil tempted him in the wilderness (Matthew 4: 1-8).

Jesus lived a fasted life. And just as he taught his disciples to pray, his words, "when you fast", reveal that he guided them through the basic rules of fasting. By saying, "when you fast" and not, "if you fast", Jesus was emphasized the inevitability of fasting to his disciples.

Jesus believed, like the Jews of his time, that fasting was a way of showing deep regret for human sin. As a result, it required definite show of outward humility and inward discipline. But he disagreed with the hypocritical show by the pharisees who fasted to attract public attention.

Jesus was often in conflict with the religious people of his time. It was clear to him that the Pharisees had become too legalistic. And in their concern for religious rituals, they had lost the spirit behind the law while insisting that the letter (interpretation of it), be obeyed.

By this public display of hypocrisy, the Pharisees missed the main purpose of worship which was to honor God and win souls to him. Their concerns instead were focused on hollow religious rites and rituals. So, Jesus decried their wrong approach to fasting.

In his incarnate nature, Jesus was a holy, righteous, and sinless man. Yet, he regarded the act of fasting as serious matter that was beyond fulfilling the demands of some religious ritual. To him, fasting involved genuine acts that touched lives for God.

So, it meant more to him than the Pharisees and the religious Jews understood it to be. It was beyond just restraining oneself from food and included the purpose to please God by abstaining from strife, anger, and oppression of the poor.

"Behold, ye fast for strife and debate, and to smite with the fist of wickedness: ye shall not fast as ye do this day, to make your voice to be heard on high. ⁵Is it such a fast that I have chosen? a day for a man to afflict his soul? is it to bow down his head as a bulrush, and to spread sackcloth and ashes under him? wilt thou call this a fast, and an acceptable day to the LORD?" (Isaiah 58: 4-5).

By regularly engaging in proper religious fasting, a believer's spirit will be transformed for good works and be ready to bear good fruit. The spirit that feeds on the word of God will be strengthened and stand firm in the face temptations.

The Holy Spirit sustained Jesus during his fast in the wilderness in ways that made him strong in the spirit even when he was weak in his physical body. This Holy Spirit will do the same for all who surrender to God through genuine fasting today.

"Fear thou not; for I am with thee: be not dismayed; for I am thy God: I will strengthen thee; yea, I will help thee; yea, I will uphold thee with the right hand of my righteousness." (Isaiah 41: 10).

As a child of faith, no believer living steadfastly in accordance to God's commandment ought to live in fear of the Devil. Obeying God's word is the key that opens the door into his presence, where no Devil can operate.

Jesus knew that obeying God's word to the letter was the secret to successful life and ministry. So, he fasted and prayed for the strength to do God's will. This duly prepared him for anything the Devil might throw at him to scuttle his mission.

As a result, he was able to easily dismiss the tempter with the simple but powerful phrase, "It is written". Under the cover of God's word and the Holy Spirit, Jesus received spiritual power during his fast that enabled him to outwit the Devil and overcome all temptations.

It is true that the Devil knows God's word. But we must not forget that Jesus is the Word of God that was made flesh. This word was Jesus' platform for prayer and fasting that helped him grow in wisdom, navigate the dark corners of this perverse world and obtain victory over sin.

Jesus would not put himself through forty grueling days of denial if fasting had no significance in his ministry. The number, forty, has a unique meaning in the Bible. It symbolizes several things, some of which are good and others bad.

In the context of Jesus' long fast, and others who went through similar challenges, the number forty generally represents trials, tests, and hardships. It is also connected to the time endured in days, months, or years, preceding a triumph or the fulfillment of God's promise.

Just as an athlete develops his muscles by training, fasting helped Jesus build strong spiritual muscles which enabled him endure trials, and persecutions in his ministry. It kept his spirit connected to the portals of power from where he received authority to save, heal, and deliver.

Fasting affords a person the time to weep for his misdeeds and to intercede for the sins of others. Jesus was a righteous man, but he denied himself the pleasures of heaven to die for human sins. This shows how honorable it is before God when a believer intercedes for others.

Jesus' humble submission through fasting was to acknowledge his insufficiency on earth before an All-sufficient God in heaven. This way, he revealed the secret of total dependence on his father without whom he could do nothing.

In a chaotic world that is perverted by sin, it is certain that no one will accomplish anything meaningful without trusting God. There will always be trials and challenges in this life. But a person who turns to God with fasts and prayers will overcome like Jesus did.

Such a Christian will have the fortitude to handle the emotions of fear, anxiety, and doubt with godly calm. The enemy's master plan is to upset a man's spirit, thereby weakening his faith when the storms of life arise. But a fasted Christian will stand strong and not be moved.

A Christian who fasts regularly will stand on his faith and flow in the power of God like Jesus did when the Devil tempted him. That person of faith never gives room for negotiation with the Devil and has no time to consider what the enemy has to offer.

Fasting tames the human spirit, making the soul and the flesh to be dependent on God in a way that puts the Devil to shame. This way, that victorious child of God receives power from God that prepares his life for godly authority, wisdom, understanding and grace for life and ministry.

A genuine fasting exercise will undoubtedly provoke an intense desire in a Christian to live a life of obedience, humility, honesty with men and compassion for weak souls. It helps in developing the Christ-like kind of love for others.

Fasting results in the purity of heart. It is a time when the mind is emptied of every ungodliness and purged of all bitterness. This enables the human spirit to have access into the cosmic realm from where it can receive divine visions and revelations.

Fasting like Jesus did will make a Christian to exhibit Christ-like virtues of love, fairness, and justice in the daily dealings with others. It will motivate a believer to show compassion to the needy, extend godly affection to the poor, and bring help to the helpless in the society.

Jesus' humble fasts resonated with God in heaven, and it made him sensitive and obedient to God's commandment. So, he was determined to do his will. But a soul that is indulgent in sin, constantly rejecting God's law will not please God even if that person fasts.

"Yea, they made their hearts as an adamant stone, lest they should hear the law and the words which the Lord of hosts hath sent in the spirit by the former prophets: therefore came a great wrath from the Lord" *(Zechariah 7:12).*

God considers the prayer and fasting of any unrepentant sinner as abomination before him. For this reason, Jesus constantly chastised the Scribes, the Pharisees, and teachers of the law and disapproved of their obnoxious exposure of hypocrisy.

But God is faithful and does not forsake the penitent cry of a humble soul and broken heart. Instead, when such people fast, he rewards them with overflowing joy, and fills the mourning hearts with gladness, peace, and cheerfulness.

"And the word of the Lord of hosts came unto me, saying, Thus saith the Lord of hosts; The fast of the fourth month, and the fast of the fifth, and the fast of the seventh, and the fast of the tenth, shall be to the house of Judah joy, and gladness, and cheerful feasts; therefore love the truth and peace" *(Zechariah 8:18-19).*

An effective fasting exercise will bring the soul into the presence of the All-Sufficient God. Such deliberate effort will usher a Christian into the uncommon spiritual realm where an abundance of divine benefits is set aside for those who seek God.

Jesus understood the impact of a genuine fast more than any Jew of his era. And he exploited this great spiritual asset in a way unmatched by the Pharisees and spiritual teachers of the law in his time whose fasts did not reflect the true, inward nature of their moral state of mind.

Jesus criticized the Scribes and the Pharisees because, though they were custodians of the law, they failed to practice its provisions such as justice, and mercy. And even when they presented themselves as clean through multiple fasts, they were full of greed and selfishness.

Their regular fasts did not positively influence the society for God neither did it help the poor. So, Jesus described them as whitewashed tombs. These tombs, Jesus said, looked beautiful on the outside, but were full of dead men's bones, inside (Matthew 23: 13-29).

Jesus deeply understood the Devil's agenda to foil any attempt by children of God to be in right standing with him. So, he prepared himself through a forty-days fast so he could deal with all those arears where the enemy had always caught believers unawares.

The devil will always test children of God in the flesh, through food, sex, alcohol. or drugs. Other arears are in the word of God as well as in material things. But Jesus' fast prepared him and enabled him to defeat the Devil in all the critical arears that the Devil tested him. (Matthew 4: 1-8).

In his human nature, Jesus was hungry and weak after fasting for forty days. But when the Devil dared him to turn stones to bread to satisfy his carnal hunger, he declined to display his divine power just to prove his sonship to the man of perdition.

As the bread of life, Jesus did not need to fast. He even, more than once, fed a multitude with a boy's lunch pack of two fish and five loaves. But he fasted regularly in his incarnate form to keep his spirit connected to his father and the source of his power.

The Devil challenged him on his knowledge of God's word during the fast. And he showed that he not only knew God's word and obeyed it, but that he was the word of God incarnate. Thus, he did not permit any frivolous challenges to distract him from fulfilling his purpose.

Jesus understood that seasons of rest must be preceded by times of labor and that greatness came only from great trials. So, he ensured that he had teeth that were cut by prayer and fasting that could handle tough issues of the kingdom.

His purpose was to redeem mankind from the bondage of sin and to destroy the works of darkness through his shed blood. That was why he left his throne in heaven and took the likeness of man to fulfill the will of his Father. (1John 3:8).

"For ye are bought with a price: therefore glorify God in your body, and in your spirit, which are God's" (1 Corinthians 6: 20).

Jesus was transparent with his disciples and mentored them by his exemplary life. He had implicit confidence in his father and encouraged his disciples to live by this example and build strong faith through ceaseless prayer and genuine fasts.

Blood-bought Christians who follow this same standard pattern of regular fasts and prayers will glorify God and accomplish Christ's purpose for their lives. They will also do greater things than Jesus did, which is his promise to his disciples.

PRAYER POINTS

1. Judgement against me from evil altars, I nullify you as I fast and pray, in Jesus' name.

2. Blood of Jesus speak for me against the powers from the coven, in Jesus' name.

3. As I fast and pray, divinations using my name, fail woefully, in Jesus' name.

4. As I fast and pray, enchantments against my life, become impotent, in Jesus' name.

5. My fasting and prayer, release me from evil soul-tie, in Jesus' name.

6. Ancient curses operating in my life, break now as I fast and pray, in Jesus' name.

7. Bread of life, sustain me as I fast and pray, in Jesus' name.

8. Holy Ghost fire consume the distractions assigned to hinder my fasting and prayer, in Jesus' name.

9. Holy Spirit, arrest my spirit, soul, and body as I fast and pray, in Jesus' name.

10. Voice of God, silence every evil voice delegated to confuse me during my fast, in Jesus' name.

11. Holy Spirit, enable me to focus on genuine motives as I fast and pray, in Jesus' name.

12. Blood of Jesus, cancel every contrary handwriting against me, as I fast and pray, in Jesus' name.

13. As I fast and pray, Holy Spirit order my desires to the right place, in Jesus' name.

14. Light of God cause my star to become a super star as I fast and pray, in Jesus' name.

CHAPTER SIX

MYTHS ABOUT FASTING

SOME OF THE GREAT STRUGGLES A CHRISTIAN WILL encounter with religious fasting involve the misrepresentations attached to it. As a result of these, many myths were created around this concept. So, to appreciate what a fast is, it is helpful to understand what it is not.

For while a fast is an incredibly religious asset and weapon of spiritual warfare, it must be understood that there are things it cannot do. Thus, no matter how it is employed, it cannot change established spiritual principles.

So, in line with the subject matter of this chapter, few myths will be discussed in this chapter (but not in any order), beginning with:

1). YOU CAN FAST WITHOUT PRAYING.

It is quite practicable and normal to pray while not fasting. But to fast without praying is a useless exercise. It is arguably impossible to engage in serious intimacy with any person when there is no meaningful communication. That is why prayer is inevitable during a fast.

Prayer represents the different ways of reaching out to God and hearing from him. So, while the motive of a fast and the sacrifices made help to establish a bond with God, prayer is the means for expressing the heart's desire and sustaining the rapport with God created during the fast.

Silence during a fast, to meditate on God's word and to hear from him, is still a manner of prayer. This is called silent prayer. Elijah prayed like this on Mount Carmel before the rain fell over Israel. So, prayer is a necessary complement of a fast.

2). FASTING CAUSES GOD TO CHANGE HIS MIND.

Fasting must not be used as a tool to manipulate God. No believer can bribe God with a fast to change his will. A person who has fasted for God's grace and mercies must be ready to accept what the will of God is concerning that situation.

Because, while fasting pleases God, it cannot make him change his mind on any matter, neither will it cause him to move his hand. No one can get all he needs because he fasted. And even when God says "no", it may be a training in understanding God' ways and timing.

It is in the interest of a Christian to fast regularly. This way, that Christian routinely and gainfully empties his heart of all carnal filthiness that daily invade the spirit man. This simple act of commonsense helps to purify the mind and maintain the sanity of the soul.

3). FASTING MAKES A BELIEVER IMMORTAL.

This is a myth. Because if it were true, servants of God like Moses, prophets Elijah and Elisha, apostles Peter,

John, Paul, and all the early disciples of Jesus, who were known to have fasted regularly, would still be alive today.

Jesus in his incarnate form fasted as regularly as he prayed. He went through all the natural challenges of life, being in the form of man. Yet, this did not make him invincible or invisible at any time during his earthly ministry. He was crucified and died like all mortal men.

4). FASTING IS A VERTICAL TRANSACTION.

While fasting is a practical display of devotion towards God who is in heaven, it calls a good measure of attention to the needy, to the poor and to the helpless who are on earth. In all sincerity, no one who does not genuinely love his neighbors can honestly say that he loves God.

Thus, the fast that will appeal to God in heaven, will first influence lives for him on earth. This is the fast that delights his heart because it meets his righteous standards. A fast will not touch God's heart in heaven if it has not positively affected souls on earth.

The man who fasts must endeavor to show kindness to the poor on earth who daily cry for hunger. He must purpose in his heart to assist the fatherless, the orphan and the helpless. And it must be his willing desire to make the widow's heart to sing for joy.

A fast that is only vertical will not yield any benefits. God will not recognize such act of faith that has no corresponding good deeds on earth. The act of faith towards God who no one can see, should be backed by acts of kindness and love to fellow creatures, who you see daily.

"Behold, ye fast for strife and debate, and to smite with the fist of wickedness: ye shall not fast as ye do this day, to make your voice to be heard on high. (Isaiah 58:4)

This scripture illustrates the value of works to God before a fast, during, and after it. But sadly, human ego, selfishness, pride, lack of dignity for humanity and wicked acts of inhumanity to the helpless, deny the legalistic mind access to God's voice.

Concerning spiritual laws, God does not compromise his standards. He insists that every man must obey his laws, commandments, statutes, and to love him. In addition, he adds that love for him was as important as love for one's neighbor.

Jesus had everything he needed in heaven. But the love to redeem perishing souls made him leave his comfort zone. And while on earth, he had compassion for mankind, and showed kindness to all before taking the place of the sinner on the cross.

"Therefore, as ye abound in everything, in faith, and utterance, and knowledge, and in all diligence, and in your love to us, see that ye abound in this grace also. I speak not by commandment, but by occasion of the forwardness of others, and to prove the sincerity of your love. For ye know the grace of our Lord Jesus Christ, that, though he was rich, yet for your sakes he became poor, that ye through his poverty might be rich." (2 Corinthians 8: 7-9)

As a man, Jesus set aside his heavenly riches, glory, and rights to provide all mankind with the gift of salvation. The blood he shed on the cross was applied to God's account to purchase redemption for believing humanity.

This way, he set a pattern which believers can copy when they fast. So, the food given up during a fast or the value of it, can be donated to change the lives of people that are struggling to survive. And the prayers of intercession can bring comfort to souls.

So, how long a fasting program lasts, the quantity or quality of food abstained from, or how intense the prayer was, will not matter to God if no one's life was blessed. Any fast that will not bring comfort to the afflicted and justice for the oppressed is worthless before God.

Jesus not only preached the gospel to the multitude daily, he healed their sick, delivered those that were bound by the Devil, and fed the hungry. He made the lame to walk, the blind to see and those who came to him never went away hungry. He touched lives.

So, he demands the show of a measurable level of compassion and love, not just to our family members and friends, but to others who may not be lovable. Every desire for intimacy with Jesus, who no man can see, must begin with intimacy with those we can see and touch.

A fast is therefore, not a mystery ladder for climbing into the throne room of God to obtain uncommon favors. It is also not a type of spiritual laser beam to see into the mind of God or a special treat to be dangled before God to make him do something he never wanted to do.

And it is neither a miracle wand with which heaven can be conjured from the earth. It is just that quality time to mourn and repent from personal sins, the sins of others, plead for forgiveness and seek for God's favors.

5). FASTING CRUSHES ALL CHALLENGES.

Myths like this debase the true meaning of a fast. Because while a fast may pull down strongholds, it is not and insurance against all human problems. The believer will experience afflictions and even spirit-filled Christians will sometimes encounter unexplainable problems in life.

Apostle Paul was known for his regular fasting habits. Yet he faced different trials during his ministry. This is evidence that fasting is not a security against hardships and afflictions. They will surely come with or without fasting.

"For we would not, brethren, have you ignorant of our trouble which came to us in Asia, that we were pressed out of measure, above strength, insomuch that we despaired even of life: But we had the sentence of death in ourselves, that we should not trust in ourselves, but in God which raiseth the dead: Who delivered us from so great a death, and doth deliver: in whom we trust that he will yet deliver us; (2 Corinthians 1: 8-10)

What a fast does however is empower the believer to accept such situations with humility and without grumbling. God is faithful and would never abandon his children in the fire of affliction. He walks them through it or comes in the appropriate time to rescue the faithful.

An obviously fasted Paul did not give details of the troubles he and his travelling companions encountered. But the doom and death they faced on these journeys showed that their survival was mainly due to the mercies of God and their trust in his comfort and grace.

6). GOD ONLY RESPONDS TO LENGHTY FASTS

This is another false spiritual opinion. Fasting is God's spiritual weapon to his children. But his response to a fast is not based on the length of the fast. God will respond to all right motives presented during a fast irrespective of the length of time applied.

"Then said he unto me, Fear not, Daniel: for from the first day that thou didst set thine heart to understand, and to chasten thyself before thy God, thy words were heard," (Daniel 10: 12).

It is on Bible record that God immediately dispatched an angel in response to Daniel's prayer from the first day of his fast. However, Moses spent forty days and forty nights on Mount Sinai before God gave him the tablets of the Law. Case of "different strokes for different folks".

"And he was there with the Lord forty days and forty nights; he did neither eat bread, nor drink water. And he wrote upon the tables the words of the covenant," (Exodus 34: 28)

7). SEX DURING A FAST IS SIN.

The major essence of a fast revolves on abstention from all forms of worldly desires that may lead to distractions. Making love, or having sex is no doubt one such many distractions. Others include time on social media, television, or cell phone.

Keeping away from these seductions is evidence of self-control. And while it is honorable before God to agree with one's spouse to avoid sex during this period, there is no specific biblical statute condemning sexual contact with a dully married spouse because of a fast.

So, to say that making love during a fast is a sin, is unscriptural. It has no biblical basis. And like all myths, it is a misguided conclusion.

PRAYER POINTS

1. Holy Spirit, deliver my star from the control of principalities and powers as I fast and pray, in Jesus' name.

2. Holy Spirit guide my star away from under dark clouds, as I fast and pray, in Jesus' name.

3. Principalities and powers shall bow to my star as I fast and pray in Jesus' name.

4. O God, divide any river that must be divided to give me access, as I fast and pray, in Jesus' name.

5. My father, dry up any river that must dry up to free my passage, as I fast and pray, in Jesus' name.

6. Way maker, make an uncommon way for me, as I fast and pray, in Jesus' name.

7. O Lord, as I fast and pray, shut up the mouths of the lions that want to devour me, in Jesus' name.

8. Prison walls surrounding my destiny, collapse and release me, as I pray and praise, in Jesus' name.

9. Powers manipulating my life from any grave, I bury you permanently, in Jesus' name.

10. Sovereign God, hear, and answer me in Jesus' name.

11. Powers contending with my glory, scatter now, as I fast and pray, in Jesus' name.

12. As I fast and pray, let the knees of my problems buckle and bow, in Jesus' name.

13. Liquid fire from heaven, melt the gates of brass holding me hostage, in Jesus' name.

14. O God, turn my ridicule into miracles, in Jesus' name.

CHAPTER SEVEN

USEFUL FASTING PROTOCOLS

BE PREPARED.

In apostle Paul's first epistle to the Corinthians, he employed the grueling preparatory methods used by athletes before a competition to illustrate the hard-work, self-denial and discipline required of anyone who intends to live a committed Christian life.

All these measures compare effectively with the necessary steps required to get oneself ready for an effective religious fast. God is overly concerned with the details put in place to build an intimate friendship, relationship, and fellowship with him.

So, following the fasting blueprint of Jesus and apostle Paul, who were two of the greatest men of prayer and fasting in the New Testament, any Christian will make impact in heaven before God and touch lives on earth, like they did.

It enabled Jesus to transform ordinary disciples into extraordinary figures. The same protocol also humbled apostle Paul with the discipline that inspired him to write more epistles in the New Testament than any Christian author of his time.

"But I keep under my body, and bring it into subjection: lest that by any means, when I have preached to others, I myself should be a castaway." (1 Corinthians 9: 27).

These factors are very essential tools for fasting too. They equip a believer to proceed and complete the process without being distracted by the thought of food, the sight of it or its smell, no matter how long the program lasts.

You will observe that fasting and prayer were two key factors that helped apostle Paul overcome difficulties and opposition in his ministry. In the face of these challenges, he fasted and prayed. These resulted in un-common turn-around of circumstances to his great advantage.

"And we being exceedingly tossed with a tempest, the next day they lightened the ship; And the third day we cast out with our own hands the tackling of the ship. And when neither sun nor stars in many days appeared, and no small tempest lay on us, all hope that we should be saved was then taken away. But after long abstinence Paul stood forth in the midst of them, and said, Sirs, ye should have hearkened unto me, and not have loosed from Crete, and to have gained this harm and loss. And now I exhort you to be of good cheer: for there shall be no loss of any man's life among you, but of the ship. For there stood by me this night the angel of God, whose I am, and whom I serve, Saying, Fear not, Paul; thou must be brought before Caesar: and, lo, God hath given thee all them that sail with thee. Wherefore, sirs, be of good cheer: for I believe God, that it shall be even as it was told me" (Acts 27: 18-25).

Anyone committed to fasting and prayer will develop a healthy spiritual, physical, and emotional lifestyle. The starting point, however, is having a clean motive, being humble, and having the desire to readily make impactful sacrifice that will please God.

God is a faithful rewarder of those who diligently seek him. He never forsakes his children or fails to respond to their cries. He is always in time to come to their rescue and to guide them victoriously through tough times (Psalm 18: 3-6).

Fasting is a serious activity that is akin to war. And the best step to engaging in any war is to get prepared for the inevitable. As a man fasts and prays, his soul gets ready to confront and deal with distractions that might surface to take away his focus.

"For which of you, intending to build a tower, sitteth not down first, and counteth the cost, whether he have sufficient to finish it? Lest haply, after he hath laid the foundation, and is not able to finish it, all that behold it begin to mock him, Saying, This man began to build, and was not able to finish. Or what king, going to make war against another king, sitteth not down first, and consulteth whether he be able with ten thousand to meet him that cometh against him with twenty thousand?" (Luke 14: 28-31).

No problem in life began the day it manifested. All problems are fruits that appear after seasons of errors in the human tree of life. Many problems may be inherited, some programmed by the enemy, but the rest are the harvests of past wrong choices.

The enemy keeps track of human mistakes in his archives. So, to deal with such errors and wipe out their records, a Christian must be well prepared. And the only way to accomplish this and recover lost grounds, is to go into higher level of spiritual warfare.

No one can effectively handle the problems in life until he has understood the source of those problems and knows how to deal with all of them. The only proven way to get to the root of human problems and deal with them is by fasting and prayer.

ESTABLISH A RIGHT MOTIVE.

A meaningful religious fast must have a right motive. This is what determines the success of a fast. The holy Spirit will help you set this up ahead of the fast. A clear motive will help a believer to stay focused and be committed during the duration of the fast.

The motive of a fast is its live wire. This is what determines the result of the fast. Every fast is a battle. And nothing benefits a child of God, whose heart is right with him, more than starting out right when going into spiritual warfare.

God is concerned with our human attitudes and motives. And when these become our priority, the sacrifices of prayer and fasting make sense to God. This is when that believer can feel the presence of God bathing him in the blood of Jesus and defending him from all evil.

"But as we were allowed of God to be put in trust with the gospel, even so we speak; not as pleasing men, but God, which trieth our hearts (1 Thessalonians 2: 4)

"The preparations of the heart in man, and the answer of the tongue, is from the LORD. All the ways of a man are clean in his own eyes; but the LORD weigheth the spirits" (Proverbs 16: 1- 2)

Some areas of focus include, but are not limited to praying for spiritual revival, bodily healing, and deliverance, for career directions, seeking for marital or financial breaks, or interceding for other Christians. Other areas are praying for spiritual gifts and for church growth.

This strategic approach helps the believer to navigate through the program without satanic bumps as the Holy Spirit is the one in control of the schedule. This way, distractions are resisted and accomplishing the intended purpose for the fast is made secure.

DETERMINE THE LENGTH OF YOUR FAST.

It is good to set a schedule before beginning a fast. But there is nothing wrong in stretching the program if the person involved is strong and is led by the Holy Spirit to do so. The health condition of the person and his spiritual viability are factors that will help determine this.

Preparations for an effective fasting program will include setting the time frame and the type of fast. Others include the books of the Bible to read, specific scriptures to memorize and meditate on, as well as when to pray, praise or rest.

When a person prepares well for a fast, he goes through it without stress, and nothing will take him by surprise.

Proper preparation is a great secret to every successful fasting. Those who apply this technique never give up along the way.

PRAYER IS IMPROTANT.

The proper role of prayer, before a fast, during, and after it cannot be underestimated. Prayer indeed, is the powerhouse behind the success of any fasting program. So, it is important to commit the program to God in prayer before it takes off.

Fasting is serious battle. If you do not pray before that battle, you will lose to the enemy even before the battle starts. But targeted prayers will strengthen the believer in every area of weakness and motivate him to kick off and coast through the fast in good mood.

Laying such a solid foundation will help to deal with obstacles that may appear during the exercise. Areas of focus during this preparatory stage include praying for good physical and emotional health, stable state of mind, and absence of stress.

A free and healthy mind will focus on Christ during a fast and not on crisis. Pray that God will transform you during the fast and equip you spiritually to influence your family in particular, the church in general and your society at large after the fast.

PRAISE WHILE YOU PRAY AND FAST.

Being in the attitude of praise helps revive the human spirit ahead of a fasting exercise. Powerful songs of praise and preparatory prayers will shape the character of the program. They send clear warning signals to the enemy that the believer is ready for battle.

Consider that it was the praise of the children of Israel, after they had circled Jericho seven times in seven days, that caused its walls to collapse. Also, the praise by Jehoshaphat's army caused the armies of Moab, Ammon, and the people of Mount Seir to destroy one another.

"And the Levites, of the children of the Kohathites, and of the children of the Korhites, stood up to praise the LORD God of Israel with a loud voice on high. And they rose early in the morning and went forth into the wilderness of Tekoa: and as they went forth, Jehoshaphat stood and said, Hear me, O Judah, and ye inhabitants of Jerusalem; Believe in the LORD your God, so shall ye be established; believe his prophets, so shall ye prosper. And when he had consulted with the people, he appointed singers unto the LORD, and that should praise the beauty of holiness, as they went out before the army, and to say, Praise the LORD; for his mercy endureth forever. And when they began to sing and to praise, the LORD set ambushments against the children of Ammon, Moab, and mount Seir, which were come against Judah; and they were smitten. For the children of Ammon and Moab stood up against the inhabitants of mount Seir, utterly to slay and destroy them: and when they had made an end of the inhabitants of Seir, everyone helped to destroy another" ((2 Chronicles 20: 19-23).

Praise in the mouth of a believer sets the tone for a victorious fast. It helps to reinforce the spiritual wall of protection surrounding that child of God. It strengthens a man's faith and eradicates the feeling of fear, while motivating the Christian to face unsavory situations with boldness.

Holy praise strikes fear into the enemy's spirit. It weakens the enemy's ability to fight a faithful child of God and erodes the enemy's boldness. It causes the enemy to surrender and flee from battle, sometimes, even before the battle begins.

STUDY GOD'S WORD AND MEDITATE ON IT.

Many Christians do not get to study God's word as much as they should. As a result, they live with a very shallow knowledge of this powerful instrument of victory and good success. The word of God is the most potent weapon of spiritual warfare.

The word of God is pure, true, and is infallible. Just as it was in the past, it is today, and shall remain forever. It is sharp and powerful, and while it can change situations, it remains unchangeable. It is a solid ground to stand on during a fast and always.

A time of fasting therefore offers a believer the opportunity to dig deep into the study of God's word, accept it, and apply it. Those who desire to know God intimately must form a lifelong, committed, daily habit of studying his word. Use it, pray it, and chew on it while you fast.

Storing up God's commands in the heart helps the Christian to be prepared when inevitable challenges of life come his way. It also helps such a believer to understand the benefits provided in his heritage in Christ. The word of God will help a person to stay out of trouble.

Life is full of many troubles that lead to heartbreaks, fears, doubts, and worrying situations. These factors keep the soul under constant stress and weaken the ability of the human body from resisting any temptations posed by worldly attractions.

The word of God, however, is full of comforting promises for those who know their God completely depend on him to ward off any seductions. In God's word, many Christians find the strength to be victorious over storms of life.

God is in ultimate control of the entire universe which he created, including man and everything that exists in it. So, when the world is in disarray and it looks like there is no hope, the Christian can go back to God's word in fasting and prayer to find peace and solace.

So, every meaningful fasting program must be time to deeply search the word of God like men search for gold in the mine. It is not just a time to read the Bible, but a consecrated time to study the scriptures in prayer, while the Holy Spirit guides the mind.

And because fasting is time alone with God, the believer should use it to get useful secrets as he studies and meditates on his word. Any version of the Bible that is easy to understand and one that the person is comfortable with will serve a good purpose.

As God's word is regularly imbibed, especially during fasting, it will make great impact on a Christian's spirit. This will lead to a marked transformation of life and to the production of abundant harvest that is beyond imagination.

"But he that received seed into the good ground is he that heareth the word, and understandeth it; which also beareth fruit, and bringeth forth, some an hundredfold, some sixty, some thirty." (Matthew 13: 23).

God's word is rich in resources that help the Christian realize his potential and be blessed. Many satanic pitfalls will be avoided in the journey of life if Christians will spend valuable time acquiring deep knowledge of God's word and getting a good understanding of it.

"This book of the law shall not depart out of thy mouth; but thou shalt meditate therein day and night, that thou mayest observe to do according to all that is written therein: for then thou shalt make thy way prosperous, and then thou shalt have good success." (Joshua 1: 8).

FOCUS ON GOD.

The basic idea behind fasting is to set time aside to connect one's human spirit with the spirit of God. So, the challenge during such a time is to take all human attention away from the world and from self and place such on God.

It is a time of some of the fiercest spiritual battles. Face the battle like David did in the Bible. He did not focus on the size of Goliath but on God. Daniel did not focus on the lions neither did the three Hebrew boys focus on the fire in the furnace. They respectively set their eyes on God.

Joseph was a seventeen-year teenager when he was sold by his brothers to Ishmaelite traders. But even in Egypt, he never forgot that his heavenly King was greater than Potiphar and Pharaoh, the king of Egypt. So, he kept his focus on God.

Religious fasting should aim at focusing on God. This keeps the mind from distractions. When distractions are not entertained, it becomes difficult to obstruct a believer's line of communication with heaven. It is then easier to hear clearly when God speaks.

The process becomes an exercise in futility when it is done to gain public approval, impress people or bring attention to self. This was the hypocrisy of the times that Jesus lived in. And he outrightly condemned the dramatics of the Pharisees that did this.

Keeping the mind completely focused on God to whom nothing is impossible also ensures that the person is not distracted by the size of the problem. It makes the mind less concerned about the situation which in the end must bow before the Almighty God.

"Behold, I am the Lord, the God of all flesh: is there anything too hard for me?" (Jeremiah 32: 27).

A mind that is focused on God will not be concerned about the raw deals of life or be attracted to the deceitfulness of human riches. It will not be drawn to a corrupt world whose unrestrained cravings grieve the heart of God.

Thus, fasting demands the cleansing of the soul of its many gods to enable the mind concentrate on the Sovereign person of God. It is a time to put away the idols of television, internet, cell phone and to maintain a righteous technological distance from the social media.

PREPARE YOUR BODY TO GO WITHOUT PHYSICAL FOOD.

Prayer and fasting are practical factors that enable the soul to experience healing, peace, prosperity, and lasting joy. Although these two disciplines can be difficult for a starter or when a person is sick and indisposed, they are powerful and extremely rewarding.

The objective of denying the flesh physical food to spend time in the presence of God is to appreciate him for his bounteous blessings. It is also to remind oneself that the flesh can live with a lot less, as long as it can continue to feed on the spiritual food, which is the word of God.

It is advisable to keep off strenuous jobs and other exercise that can drain the energy or stress physical muscles during a fast. Stay away from the kitchen, refrigerator, medications (except on medical advice), caffeinated drinks and alcohols.

CONSIDER OTHERS.

While a man's major duties in life include the fear of God, serving him and seeking intimacy with him, God's added supreme desire is for Christians to cultivate the habit of caring for the helpless. Whoever does this will enjoy God's relationship at a highest possible level.

It is important for a Christian to seek intimacy with God and desire to have high spiritual experiences. But such steps ought to be combined with outward acts that delight the heart of God. Human piety and empty religious rituals are not enough.

The Bible reminds believers to do good and reach out sacrificially to those who do not have. This reflects Christ's character of sacrifice that took him to the cross for the underserving. Sharing what a person has with others is the kind of selfless act of charity that pleases God.

Interceding for others is an opportunity to do what the Christian often relegates to the back burner of his religious exercises. God loves those who are eyes to the blind, feet to the lame, voices to the voiceless and the poor in our society.

Such random acts of kindness shown especially to the suffering, poor, the helpless and the hopeless make a huge difference in a hurting world. So, the Christian must learn to share what he has with others who do not have.

The Bible teaches how hospitality and compassion, no matter how small, delight God's heart. So, it is godly for his children to practice these novel arts. And by putting aside all human sulkiness, the Christian who wants to be like Christ, will find souls who need love and care.

Until a believer's concern for others becomes a major motivation for fasting, that program remains a mere selfish idea. Anyone can pray or fast all they can. But without tangible corresponding sacrifice comparable to the ritual's efforts, the exercise will not yield any positive result.

Before God, the best expression of faith is the extension of charity and affection to the less privileged. This involves caring for people who will never be capable of doing anything in return for you, or who will never be able to repay your hospitality.

"What doth it profit, my brethren, though a man say he hath faith, and have not works? can faith save him? If a brother or sister be naked, and destitute of daily food, And one of you say unto them, Depart in peace, be ye warmed and filled; notwithstanding ye give them not those things which are needful to the body; what doth it profit? Even so faith, if it hath not works, is dead, being alone." (James 2: 14—17).

A godly fast seeks to bear fruit that affects the lives of others. And God is watchful to see those radical acts of charity extended to the poor and the genuine works of compassion to the oppressed. When these are combined with faith, they smell like sweet incense to God during a fast.

So, the Christian must use his fast as a time to give back to others and not only to receive from God. Jesus ate nothing the entire time he was on trial for the sake of human sins, till he was crucified. This act of love cemented his relationship with his father.

To connect to that level of intimacy with Jesus, one must surrender something of value that can bless others. Until a person pays a price that can cancel the pain and suffering of the helpless, his fasting and prayer will make no sense.

God is pleased when what is given up during a fast serves the need of the poor. In God's kingdom, he places a high priority on the poor and the oppressed. And many such hungry and homeless people with no clothes can be found on our streets.

No help rendered to this group of people can compare to the price Jesus paid on the cross to purchase redemption for mankind. Jesus gave up his life without complaint in obedience to his father's command. The Christian will do well to pay some price too.

The Bible model stated by the prophet in Isaiah chapter 58 did not state all the godly requirements of a meaningful fasting. But it provided some helpful guidelines that can serve as a springboard to any serious-minded Christian who intends to embark on a fast.

"Behold, ye fast for strife and debate, and to smite with the fist of wickedness: ye shall not fast as ye do this day, to make your voice to be heard on high. Is it such a fast that I have chosen? a day for a man to afflict his soul? is it to bow down his head as a bulrush, and to spread sackcloth and ashes under him? wilt thou call this a fast, and an acceptable day to the LORD? Is not this the fast that I have chosen? to loose the bands of wickedness, to undo the heavy burdens, and to let the oppressed go free, and that ye break every yoke? Is it not to deal thy bread to the hungry, and that thou bring the poor that are cast out to thy house? when thou seest the naked, that thou cover him; and that thou hide not thyself from thine own flesh? Then shall thy light break forth as the morning, and thine health shall spring forth speedily: and thy righteousness shall go before thee; the glory of the LORD shall be thy rereward." (Isaiah 58: 4-8).

Many fasts start on a wrong premise because people focus more on themselves and less on others. The God-approved fast however, places priority on other human issues above this consideration. This is a better path to delight God's heart during a fast.

A Christian ought to use his fast as a time to help others. This way, he expresses that attribute of God which he inherited by creation. Christians must be determined to show love, kindness and affection to the loveless not to attract attention, but because it is the right thing to do.

Even in the Old Testament Bible, God condemned any fast that did not positively influence the destitute, the helpless, the widows and those who need to taste the love of God. In the New Testament as well, Jesus taught that acts of kindness shown to the needy, were done to him.

So, the believer honors God by going beyond himself to put others in consideration during his fast. Simply expressing those common values shared with God means a lot to him. He never overlooks this but does respond through his many graces.

Those who claim to love God, respect, and fear him, must show these by loving one another. No one can say he honors God and fails to fit into his model of love for others. God shared what he had with the world. The Christian should be able to share what he has too.

Jesus had compassion for the multitude and cared for the hungry. He not only fed them with spiritual food but ensured they did not leave his presence hungry. He shared the little he had to feed the hungry. A good Christian is expected to do the same. (Matthew 15: 30-36).

Such significant and deliberate acts of Christlike generosity during a fast matter immensely to God. They go a long way to provoke the many spiritual and physical benefits reserved for the obedient, humble, and faithful children of God.

"Then shalt thou call, and the LORD shall answer; thou shalt cry, and he shall say, Here I am. If thou take away from the midst of thee the yoke, the putting forth of the finger, and speaking vanity; And if thou draw out thy soul to the hungry, and satisfy the afflicted soul; then shall thy light rise in obscurity, and thy darkness be as the noon day: And the LORD shall guide thee continually, and satisfy thy soul in drought, and make fat thy bones: and thou shalt be like a watered garden, and like a spring of water, whose waters fail not. And they that shall be of thee shall build the old waste places: thou shalt raise up the foundations of many generations; and thou shalt be called, The repairer of the breach, The restorer of paths to dwell in." (Isaiah 58: 9-12).

There are always rewards for good works done by any Christian in the name of Christ and for God's kingdom. God does not forget such acts of love done by his children who yield themselves as instruments to fulfill his divine purpose.

ENDING A FAST.

Ending a fast is as important as starting one. It needs to be planned to avoid problems after the fast. Once the body is denied food for some time, the digestive system adapts to the change. Common sense and science dictate that reintroduction of food must be gradual.

It is advisable to start with warm liquids, fruits, salads, and other vegetables. This can be followed subsequently with light solids which should be introduced in small portions. This will help the process of recovering strength and regaining good physical health.

It is also important to maintain the benefits of a person's fasting program. Therefore, remember to keep up with regular quiet-time with God, to read the Bible daily, meditate on God's word regularly and listen to hear when God is speaking and what he is saying.

Fasting is keeping serious appointment with God. So, the benefits must not be lost by engaging again in acts of unrighteousness. Remember not to fall for the attraction of old habits. Be careful and diligent because the Devil will come in different shades and colors to tempt you.

PRAYER POINTS

1. My prayers in this fast will shake the doors and windows of heaven, in Jesus' name.

2. As I fast and pray, stumbling blocks before me shall become the steppingstones to my higher ground, in Jesus' name.

3. As I fast and pray, doors of righteousness, peace, and joy in the Holy Ghost shall open unto me, in Jesus' name.

4. Holy Spirit, make my words a source of comfort to those around me, in Jesus' name.

5. My father, in this fast, anoint my head with oil and cause my cup to run over, in Jesus' name.

6. O God, as I fast and pray, release eternal blessings upon my life, in Jesus' name.

7. Let my fast and prayers usher me into the presence of God, in Jesus' name.

8. Let my fast and prayers release the dew of heaven upon my labor, in Jesus' name.

9. Holy Spirit, give me peace that surpasses all understanding as I fast and pray, in Jesus' name.

10. O Lord, give me strength for every battle as I fast and pray, in Jesus' name.

11. As I fast and pray, O God, do not be silent to my pain, in Jesus' name.

12. As I fast and pray, do not be blind to my tears O God, in Jesus' name.

13. My father, deliver me from the reproach of men and women, in Jesus' name.

14. My father, give me a booster dose of your power, as I fast and pray, in Jesus' name.

CHAPTER EIGHT

HINDERANCES TO GENIUNE FASTING

FOCUSING ON FOOD.

THE PRIMARY ESSENCE OF A FAST IS TO DENY THE PHYSICAL body natural food while the soul is fed with spiritual food. Anyone fasting must keep his attention away from food. Thoughts about food, or drinks during a fast will distract the mind and weaken the body.

A believer's attention during a fast should be focused on God and not on natural comforts. Concentrating on God and the things above will enable the mind to experience the power, love, joy, and peace that God lavishes on all who come into his presence.

The Devil understands that hunger can weaken a soul during the fast. And he will use the smell, sight, or image of food as weapons to weaken the flesh and frustrate that program. So, endeavor to keep the mind numbed against food when you fast.

REPENT FROM EVERY WICKEDNESS.

Fasting must begin with genuine act of repentance from sin and a turning to God. The individual, who desires to fast must put away all evil habits that estrange him from God. It is the spiritual duty of the Christian to abstain from every act of wickedness.

Hunger for reconciliation with God, the utter hatred for all sins, and the determination to forsake evil habits must be the essential motives behind any plan to fast. Without these factors, the effort will not bear good results.

A fast must be channeled towards developing and or sustaining the right attitude of living with God and man. It must shun all evil, avoid strife, and keep away from every ungodliness. This will help any soul to literally walk its way into the heart of God.

Those who desire to draw near to God must realize that he is a holy being. It is his desire also that his children be holy as he is. This godly desire for human righteousness must be the believer's concern. This will help a Christian to flee from every appearance of evil.

Every wrong moral attitude, depravity or evil disposition will annul the promise of God to bless those who walk blameless before him. But he will not withhold any good thing from the righteous believer who diligently seeks his face. (Genesis 17:1; Psalm 84:12).

There must be a human hunger for a righteous living that is devoid of any trace of wickedness. When this hunger is satisfied, it restores a right relationship with God that causes him to a reveal his righteousness in man. This certainly leads to right relationships with others too.

A soul that is cleansed from wickedness is rich in Christlike virtues of love, kindness, compassion, and generosity. And when such a believer turns to the living

God in fasting, his hungry soul, weak and tired body, is soon refreshed in a spiritual way.

UNFORGIVENESS.

People who are unwilling or unable to others for hurting them will not receive forgiveness from God. Sincerely giving up all resentments and pardoning those who have wronged you while seeking forgiveness from those you have hurt is a good step to take before any fast.

Taking such wonderful steps help to create purity of heart, a clean conscience and prepares a soul for a genuine encounter with a holy God. Ability to Forgive others is a primary step to earning God's forgiveness. It provides a natural man the moral basis to stand before a righteous God,

Every believer in the faith must develop a forgiving character. It is a great virtue that God demands from his children. Refusing to pardon is an act of disrespect, dishonor and disobedience to God who sent his Son to shed his blood for the cleansing of human sins.

The hunger for God which the believer desires during a fast must cause him to overcome every unforgiveness and hate in his own heart and cause him to put away bitterness against others. This will make room in his heart for what matters to God, such as showing kindness to the poor and the oppressed.

God wants to live in an intimate relationship with his children. But this will not happen where there are acts of unforgiveness. Believers who harbor resentment against others cannot be God's friends and they will not qualify for his mercy.

Repentance from sins and granting clemency to others are great keys to beneficial fasting. Without these important factors, a fast will be vain exercise and wasted effort. That kind of program will not yield any spiritual benefit.

Pardoning others is not an easy thing as it can be hard to forgive. But the cross is a perpetual reminder of the agony that Jesus endured so that God can forgive human sins. So, forgiveness comes from a transformed spirit. And it shows strength and not weakness, as many consider the act.

And God views the act of forgiveness so seriously that no believer with an unpardoning spirit can have access to the gates of heaven. So, he expects all Christians to forgive others, lay aside any grievance, hurts and the desire for vengeance, so that they too can receive pardon.

The holy God is loving and kind. And he forgives the sinner who asks for pardon. Not to justify sin, but to give the sinner another chance at life. Even when he reproves a sinner in his wrath, it is in righteous indignation against the sin and not the sinner.

Every Christian must learn to forgive like God who pardons all that turn back to him. He forgives their sins, restores relationship with him and revives the souls of those who cry out to him, giving them another opportunity to make a fresh start in life.

Unforgiveness destroys interpersonal, human relationships as well as the friendship with God. But the Christian who appreciates the painful suffering that Christ endured to purchase his own pardon will be willing to pardon others who have hurt him, even as Christ forgave his sins.

God relates better with his children when they obey his word and operate in the likeness of his holy character. He is a loving, kind and compassionate being who willingly freed man from all his debts. And he desires that everyone be willing to free those who have wronged them.

No Christian can go to God with a dirty, unforgiving heart and expect any good response. Unforgiveness is the root of bitterness that bear the fruit of anger, and hate. These will make a Christian to fall short of God's glory and must be destroyed.

"Lest there should be among you man, or woman, or family, or tribe, whose heart turneth away this day from the LORD our God, to go and serve the gods of these nations; lest there should be among you a root that beareth gall and wormwood; And it come to pass, when he heareth the words of this curse, that he bless himself in his heart, saying, I shall have peace, though I walk in the imagination of mine heart, to add drunkenness to thirst:" (Deuteronomy 29: 18-19).

"Follow peace with all men, and holiness, without which no man shall see the Lord: Looking diligently lest any man fail of the grace of God; lest any root of bitterness springing up trouble you, and thereby many be defiled;" (Hebrews 12: 14-15).

Dealing with the unforgiving spirit qualifies a Christian to receive forgiveness from God. In this cleansed condition, the child of God who is now working in obedience to the terms of God's covenant relationship becomes firmly re-rooted in Christ.

Efforts in fasting and prayer become useless when they do nothing to improve human behavior in ways that reflect the nature of God. God is not interested in mere religious rituals based on emotions and teachings of human doctrines.

He knows how fragile the human nature has become due to sin. He is more concerned with the righteousness of his spirit than with the piety of his empty religion. And he knows that by forgiving others, the believer reflects that image of God in which he was formed.

To forgive mankind of their sins, God provided the ultimate sacrifice by offering his only Son to die on the cross. There, Jesus shed his blood for the remission of human sins. So, those who receive this mercy should be willing to extend it to others as God did for them. (Zechariah 7:1-7).

STRIFE.

Every person of faith must be capable of reflecting Christlike virtues even in a world that is opposed to godly love and peace. The Christian is the light of God on earth. So, he must shine in this world in a way that will enable others see the character of Christ in him.

That way, the light of God will reach the dark places of the earth and cause peace to reign there over chaos. This might seem a difficult thing to accomplish in a troubled world, yet it is not impossible for people to live peacefully without striving against one another.

God will not respond to any sacred efforts that are laced with strife, murmuring, grumbling, and disputing attitudes which are the root causes of divisiveness amongst his children. And except a soul has dominion over these issues, it will not have access into the presence of God.

"Good and upright is the LORD: therefore will he teach sinners in the way" (Psalm 25:8).

Afflicting the soul under any unrighteous conditions will not attract God's attention. Thus, a fast becomes futile when a heart overcome with bitterness and strife goes to God in prayer. Such vices are evil padlocks that block the believer's way to his higher ground.

Every Christian is expected to regularly bear good fruit. This is evidence of righteousness and spiritual growth in that life. But fighting and strife will not permit this growth. And except for the good fight of faith, faith and fight should not dwell in the same heart.

THE LYING HABIT

God's standard for a relationship with his children is established in the Bible. It is clearly stated there that every transgression is evil before him and that he hates all sins with perfect hatred. This is part of the few conditions for walking with him.

But of all transgressions before the eyes of a holy God, lying is one of the most contemptible because its source is from the kingdom of darkness. As the climax of all sins, lying is linked to Satan, who is the father of all liars.

Lying is among the seven sins considered to be most deadly in the Bible. In that scripture in Proverbs written by King Solomon, it appears in two forms. First as a lying tongue, and next as a false witness that is speaks lies.

"For your hands are defiled with blood, and your fingers with iniquity; your lips have spoken lies, your tongue hath muttered perverseness" (Isaiah 59: 3).

The other five deadly sins include: a proud look, hands that shed innocent blood, heart that devices wicked imaginations, feet that are swift in running to mischief, and he who sows discord among his brethren. All these are said to be abominable to God.

Every motive of a liar is dishonest, and deceptive and is tailored towards putting God's children into bondage. All believers are made in the image of God who is incapable of lying. As a result, God does not expect his children to be liars. A Christian liar will grieve the Holy Spirit.

Liars have "deceptive tongue" and can easily confuse any gullible Christian. From the beginning of creation, the devil proved that he was a liar. He deceived Adam and Eve and taught them how to lie. But now all Christians are indwelt by the Holy Spirit who teaches them the truth.

A liar will never experience the grace of God. And because he lacks the character of truth, which is from God, any sacrifice he makes in prayer or fasting is regarded as abomination before the righteous God who sees the heart of all men (Proverbs 15: 8).

DISOBEYING GOD'S WORD.

The greatest accomplishment of every true Christian is to obey God and do his commandment. No disobedient Christian can call himself a child of God. An errant believer runs the great risk of falling into danger, like prophet Jonah.

Merely hearing God's word is not enough for any Christian to make heaven. What matters is that the Christian who hears the word must be a doer of it. You do not argue, doubt, delay, or obey partially. You swiftly obey every letter as God said it.

The fast and prayers of a rebellious Christian are abomination to a righteous God. Disobedience to God's laws, commandments and statutes undermine every motive of prayer. They render the objective of any fast purposeless and its sacrifice, useless.

THE FAST AS A BRIBE FACTOR.

No one can bribe God, and bribery is condemned in the Bible. So, it is ungodly to use a fast as bribe to God. David was "a man after God's heart". He was a person who could get whatever he asked from God. But after he sinned and tried to use his fast as a bribe, God rebuffed him. (2 Samuel 12: 20-33).

In the law of Moses, God forbade the giving and taking of a bribe. In the Bible, bribery is considered a sin because it leads to twisting of judgment and the perversion of justice. Thus, the one who gives a bribe is as guilty as the receiver. (Exodus 23: 8; Deuteronomy 16: 19).

SHOWING OFF WITH YOUR FAST.

In Judaism, the Pharisees were a sect of religious Jews. Apart from the regular sacred fasts on the days of the religious feasts prescribed by the Law of Moses, the

Pharisees also fasted two times every week as a sign of their religious piety.

Jesus was critical of their approach. And he condemned them not because they fasted, but how they conducted themselves during their fasts. Their outward display of worship was mainly for public spectacle, an adulation which God does not reward.

FORCED FASTING.

A fast loses its real meaning when it is forced on an unwilling soul. Such a reluctant act will lack purpose and cannot produce any benefits because it was not deliberate. In this situation, there will be no motivation to make any worthy sacrifice.

A fast can only be meaningful when it is thoughtfully planned and prayerfully executed. God will not punish any Christian who fails to fast. But then, such a believer will be powerless and can easily fall prey to the devil.

No child of God should wait until they are forced by a problem to engage in a fast. Two incidents in the bible come to mind. The first is the case of David, a man well beloved by God and who God described as a man after his heart.

Most of the psalms confirm that David was a man of prayer. But beyond that, there is no record that he fasted often, except perhaps during the regular temple fasts. Prayer is a good path to finding God. But there are situations in life when prayer alone will not serve the purpose.

The only record of extra fasting in David's life was

when the boy born out of the adultery with Bathsheba, Uriah's wife, was sick. Then, he fasted for seven days. This type of fasting is selfish and will not attract God's favorable attention from God. No wonder that child died.

It is easy for a Christian to wander far away from the presence of God when there are no spiritual checks. That kind of Christian will be vulnerable to the Devil as the doors to his life will be wide open, making invasion by sin easy.

Fasting will always appear difficult to those who do not have the habit to refresh their relationship with God. This category of believers who only use this weapon as a rapid response measure of reaching God, never find him.

In the second incident, Jonah was forced to embark on a three-day prayer and fasting program, probably because he had no options left. Disobedience to divine instruction put him in such a very tight corner he resorted to prayer and fasting.

Many believers are like that. Their fasting never starts until there is a big problem. And because fasting has never been part of their worship agenda, the only time they consecrate a fast is when they are literarily in the belly of a fish.

These group of Christians often wait until they start drowning before they can learn how to swim. This is a bad way of life, considering that the enemy is always on duty, roaming about like a hungry lion that is seeking whom to devour.

The devil will not hesitate to sieve any victim like wheat. He will even dare to harass a Christian whose spirit, soul, and body are on Holy Ghost fire, not to mention that lazy believer whose prayer and fasting altars have no fire.

Daniel was a man accustomed to prayer and fasting. Yet, this did not deter the enemy from setting him up for destruction. But because he was prepared ahead for such moment, he did not have to pray again in the den of lions. Same goes for Apostle Paul and his companion, Silas.

PRAYER POINTS

1. Every distraction to my prayer and fasting be destroyed, in Jesus' name.

2. Holy Spirit enable me to structure my prayer and fasting on genuine motives, in Jesus' name.

3. Holy Spirit, empower me with crazy faith for ministry, in Jesus' name.

4. My father, help me fulfill the dreams you prepared for me, in Jesus' name.

5. My father, as I face "this problem", walk through it with me, in Jesus' name.

6. O Lord, help me not to ignore what you revealed to me, in Jesus' name.

7. O God, as I fast and pray, make crystal clear to me the things that were blurred before my natural eyes, in Jesus' name.

8. As I fast and pray, Holy Spirit enable me to overcome what seemed insurmountable to me, in Jesus' name.

9. My father, as I fast and pray, release to me the inheritance that cannot fade, in Jesus' name.

10. O Lord, disgrace the co-conspirators against me, as I fast and pray, in Jesus' name.

11. Sovereign God, let the door of your presence be opened to me as I fast and pray, in Jesus' name.

12. O God, as I fast and pray, let my contrite heart and broken spirit receive your mercy, in Jesus' name.

13. My father, as I fast and pray let my helpless situation receive your divine attention, in Jesus' name.

14. Man of war, as I fast and pray, go before me and smite my enemies, in Jesus' name.

CHAPTER NINE

WHEN YOU FAST

FASTING IS A DELIBERATE ACTION IN THE LIFE OF A PERSON that recognizes his desperate need for God. It is an act that causes a man's soul to focus attention on God for a reasonable time. This results in victories that are the outcome of God's goodwill.

However, while a fast has numerous benefits, it is important that the motives are not based on the miracles expected, but on the desire to experience a lasting spiritual encounter with God. When this is the priority, other things that were not even expected simply fall into place.

"But seek ye first the kingdom of God, and his righteousness; and all these things shall be added unto you" (Matthew 6: 33).

The Bible speaks eloquently about the concept of fasting in the Old Testament. And Jesus specifically mentioned it in the New Testament to his disciples, setting the clear basis for Christians to continue with this sacred practice even in the new dispensation.

Thus, Jesus' teaching in the gospels amplifies the need to fast, and to do so rightly. In that message, Jesus did not just suggest or recommend a fast as manner of worship but commanded its necessity to his disciples because of its numerous spiritual benefits.

Unlike the discipline of prayer which he taught them following a request by his disciples, Jesus knew that fasting was another powerful tool for accomplishing greater supernatural feats which they did not have. So, he taught them the right steps, saying, "Moreover when you fast".

The Bible indeed commands God's children to fast. It also teaches that genuine fasting habits delight God's heart and has its many rewards. Jesus fasted the right way during his time on earth. No wonder he had the moral boldness to rebuke those who treated a fast as fanfare.

"Moreover when ye fast, be not, as the hypocrites, of a sad countenance: for they disfigure their faces, that they may appear unto men to fast. Verily I say unto you, They have their reward. But thou, when thou fastest, anoint thine head, and wash thy face; That thou appear not unto men to fast, but unto thy Father which is in secret: and thy Father, which seeth in secret, shall reward thee openly." (Matthew 6: 16-18).

The hypocrisy mentioned in this scripture was in stern rebuke to the Pharisees who fasted twice a week to impress the public with their piety. So, Jesus condemned such spiritual displays which were done with the wrong motives.

To the contrary, the Bible teaches that the believer's fast focus on finding and doing God's will, rather than seeking for human attention. The true worship which God demands and deserves is that which is done in the secret. That is the best way of attracting his attention.

Jesus had a responsible and intimate relationship with God, and he exhibited all his attributes. He was loving, kind, obedient and had deep compassion for lost souls. Any believer who desires such intimacy with God should copy this model before, during, and after his fast.

Obeying God's commandment always delights his heart. That is why he did not hesitate to testify about this concerning Jesus, when he said, "This is my beloved son in whom I am well pleased". Thus, everyone who follows this pattern of love and kindness will also receive a testimony from God.

"And the King shall answer and say unto them, Verily I say unto you, In as much as ye have done it unto one of the least of these my brethren, ye have done it unto me" (Matthew 25: 40).

Any believer who expects attention from God during his fast will go beyond the mere ritual of afflicting his soul to show genuine compassion to the poor. So, it is not only by fixating on what one can get from God during a fast that matters, but by doing what will benefit the less privileged.

When you fast, vow to surrender somethings of value to God. These include but are not limited to natural foods and worldly pleasures. Blessing the poor must also be of high priority. There is nothing anyone can give to God that can compare to what he gave to the world.

Be honest as you can be during a fast and after it. Using Sacred religious ordinances such as sabbaths and fasts as time to postpone acts of wickedness is evil before God. This was the situation during the reign of king Herod Agrippa when the church was under serious persecution.

About that time, Herod had murdered James the brother of John with the sword. And because he saw that it pleased the Jews, he also arrested Peter. But as it was during the days of the unleavened bread, he remanded him in prison for execution after the Passover.

In ancient Israel, the Passover was the major feast of Judaism. And all Jews were required by law to fast during this period. So, the religious leaders came up with the idea to postpone the murder an innocent man, till after the fast. This was the height of religious hypocrisy.

Jezebel even did a worst thing than Herod during the reign of King Ahab. She called a fast and arranged for Naboth to be seated between two scoundrels who falsely accused him. This wicked plot led to the arrest, and gruesome murder of Naboth whose vineyard King Ahab possessed.

When you fast, let it be a sobber moment and time for weeping for your sins, mourning your mistakes, expressing affection for God, and reaffirming loyalty to him. A fast must not be occasion to reinvent evil plans or finetune acts of wickedness.

So, when you fast, humble your soul before God, turn your attention away from every carnal and material challenges. And no matter the size of any "mountain" before you, be determined to focus on God who is bigger than any problem.

In Old Testament Judaism, going without food and water, tearing of one's clothes, wearing of sackcloth, sitting in ashes, and putting ash on the head were some signs of fasting. It was a time for expressing remorse for human sins and seeking the face of a gracious God.

But the scriptures reveal that God expects more from his children during a fast than just these carnal, outward displays of penitence that were not backed by genuine inward repentance. So, the God-approved fast is the one that leads to the rending of the heart and not the garment.

"Therefore also now, saith the LORD, turn ye even to me with all your heart, and with fasting, and with weeping, and with mourning: And rend your heart, and not your garments, and turn unto the LORD your God: for he is gracious and merciful, slow to anger, and of great kindness, and repenteth him of the evil" (Joel 2: 12-13).

God wants his children to turn to him while there is time. He is gracious and merciful, slow to anger, and of great kindness. The time set aside for a fast must be properly spent reconciling and returning to God. It must be well utilized for doing good works and not for committing evil.

Jesus taught his disciples not to fast like hypocrites. The reference here was to the Pharisees who regularly practiced ceremonial cleanness but were dishonest in the heart. So, he condemned their saintly hypocrisy because their inward parts were corrupt and unclean.

"Woe unto you, scribes and Pharisees, hypocrites! for ye make clean the outside of the cup and of the platter, but within they are full of extortion and excess. Thou blind Pharisee, cleanse first that which is within the cup and platter, that the outside of them may be clean also. Woe unto you, scribes and Pharisees, hypocrites! for ye

are like unto whited sepulchres, which indeed appear beautiful outward, but are within full of dead men's bones, and of all uncleanness. Even so ye also outwardly appear righteous unto men, but within ye are full of hypocrisy and iniquity" (Matthew 23: 25-28).

He also taught that fasting should be a discrete act. Thus, except it is a general, cooperate or public fast, the social media should not be an arena for a Christian fast. Bragging about that fast and making a spectacle of your piety makes you a modern-day Pharisee. Let it be between you and God.

Moreover, when you fast", do not to be of a sad countenance, but anoint your head, and wash your face, so you are not seen by men to be fasting. Do not keep a miserable look only because of a fast. Cheer up. It is the heart that God is looking at, not the face. (Matthew 16: 16-18).

The motive of an honest fast must be to attract God and grow up spiritually and not to show off to the public. So, when you fast, use your time to empty your soul of the world, to grow in grace, and to create room for Holy Spirit to possess you in higher dimensions.

A time of fasting is when a soul can seriously imbibe God's word, assimilate it, and meditate on it. Nothing compares with the incredible knowledge gained during such moments. This comes with spiritual power, joy, and peace.

However, "when you fast", also be ready to face the Devil as much as being prepared to encounter the Lord. The Devil will be there right from the beginning to discourage or frustrate the fast. And where these attempts fail, he will strike at another opportune moment, like he did with Jesus.

The Devil knows when a person's flesh is weak and tired during a fast. And he will storm that mind with physical, spiritual, and material trials to rattle his faith. This is when the gains of a devoted Christian life should kick-in.

"When you fast", the motive should be right. The inward attitude must be pure, and the outward actions be right towards God and men. That way, "your father who is in secret; and who sees in the secret, will reward you".

The act of fasting can be tough on the body especially when it is an extended program, but it is the most practical way to show loyalty to the sovereign God and appreciate your dependence on him. It is also a way to sincerely express spiritual hunger for him and receive spiritual gifts.

The greatest joy any child of God can find is in the presence of God. When a Christian finds himself in the presence of God through his fast, he begins to see things differently. He no longer sees things through the eyes of the natural man but perceives them from the eternal perspective.

Daniel was knowledgeable in the Torah. And from studying it, he understood by the holy books that God would not allow the captives of Israel to return to their land until the seventy years spoken of by the prophets, for the desolation of Jerusalem, was accomplished.

As a true prophet who believed in God's word, when he realized, by the books that the time had come, he took God to task on his word and started a twenty-one day fast.

What he did all this time was plead with God to fulfil his promise so that his children can return to their land.

He was an acclaimed prayer warrior who often fasted. So, he began by confessing his sins, the sins of his people and to plead for God's mercy. He was certain that if God granted them mercy, which he and his people did not deserve, he would restore them. (Daniel 9: 3-4).

So, "When you fast", be honest, truthful and admit your sins and the transgressions of your ancestors like Daniel did. Daniel did not just focus on the deliverance which he sought through his fast, but also desired to know the deliverer.

In humility, he acknowledged the righteousness of God's judgment on his people, brought about by their sins and prayed that God would grant him his request according to His name's sake. And after he presented his request before God, he waited patiently to hear from him. (Daniel 9: 19).

Like Daniel, Jesus also often paired the spiritual arts of fasting and prayer in his contacts and communications with his heavenly Father. He recognized the synergy this combination brings, not only into godly living, but into spiritual warfare.

As Jesus' disciples keenly watched their master's spiritual routines, they observed the role of prayer in his daily life. And because they realized that his power was connected to his prayer-life, they asked him to teach them to pray. And he did (Matthew 6: 5-15; Luke 11: 1-4.)

Jesus made his disciples to realize the importance of prayer. But beyond just revealing the art and necessity of prayer to them, he taught them to be persistent when they pray. The Christian must never give up in prayer until the answer is received (Luke 18: 1).

Jesus knew that fasting is a sacred tool that is not only unique the Jewish religion but an important instrument of divine worship. Thus, he laid a proper foundation of this concept for his followers to ensure that they do not abuse the practice like the Pharisees of his time.

PRAYER POINTS

1. Every gathering of the wicked against my life, scatter as I fast and pray, in Jesus' name.

2. My fasting and prayer, expose and destroy my "Haman", in Jesus' name.

3. Whirlwind of God, destroy any power that says fasting, and prayer will not solve my problems, in Jesus' name.

4. Fire of God, expose and consume the spiritual ambush laid for me, in Jesus' name.

5. Spirits of misery and despair shall not frustrate my fasting and prayer, in Jesus' name.

6. I receive the anointing for good speed as I fast and pray, in Jesus' name.

7. Holy Spirit, restore my spiritual senses as I fast and pray, in Jesus' name.

8. Umbrella of darkness hindering my divine blessings, be roasted by fire, as I fast and pray, in Jesus' name.

9. My star, move out of from the evil cloud as I begin to fast and pray, in Jesus' name.

10. O God, rescue me as I fast and pray, in Jesus' name.

11. O Lord, grant me uncommon favor as I fast and pray, in Jesus' name.

12. Anointing of God break my yoke as I fast and pray, in Jesus' name.

13. My enemies shall obey me as I fast and pray, in Jesus' name.

14. Hailstones from heaven fight for me as I fast and pray, in Jesus' name.

CHAPTER TEN

FASTING AND PRAYER

THE MOST POWERFUL WEAPONS OF SPIRITUAL WARFARE available to any believer are found in the word of God. One highly effective tool in this armory is prayer. Warriors who are conversant with this spiritual missile never miss their target.

The early church leaders had no weapons beyond the word of God. And because they relied on this word and prayed, it was said that they literally turned their world upside down. It was their means of combat against their enemies, and deep source of communication with God.

Their prayers were fervent as they were factual and led to several significant results during those fragile and dark days of the infant church. Those bold and fearless disciples gave themselves up to effective prayer, all to the glory of God.

Their powerful prayers undoubtedly touched many lives, and numerous converts witnessed miracles as the disciples literally moved mountains in the name of Jesus. Thus, fervent prayer has remained a useful weapon in every area of spiritual warfare.

So, it is unquestionable that prayer in its many forms can open the doors of God's throne room for a believer to access many blessings. This notwithstanding, there are some problems that can defy prayer when it is applied as an independent instrument of worship.

Fervent prayer is indisputably a powerful spiritual arsenal in the Christian's armory. But sadly, only few of Christians understand the advantage of combining the benefits of prayer with other helpful spiritual factors of worship and warfare.

One of these many useful factors is a religious fast. When prayer is combined in a meaningful way with a religious fast, the result achieved is way beyond what any Christian would accomplish if he employed them as separate tools of worship or warfare.

Incorporating a fast to a prayer session was Jesus' secret to dealing with difficult challenges. Jesus understood the menace of unprecedented challenges. And he knew that dealing with such difficult problems required unprecedented measures.

"Then came the disciples to Jesus apart, and said, Why could not we cast him out? And Jesus said unto them, Because of your unbelief: for verily I say unto you, If ye have faith as a grain of mustard seed, ye shall say unto this mountain, Remove hence to yonder place; and it shall remove; and nothing shall be impossible unto you. Howbeit this kind goeth not out but by prayer and fasting" (Matthew 17: 19-21).

In spiritual warfare, it is hard to find any combination of weapons more powerful than fasting and prayer. When they are expertly combined in worship, they produce a more powerful effect than any one of them would have yielded separately.

The benefits of prayer cannot be undervalued. This explains why a praying Christian is described as a powerful Christian. They are the most dreaded of all believers because when their holy, violent prayers combine with a holy fast, heaven is set on high alert, and hell goes in disarray.

A good blend of scriptural prayer with a genuine fast will literarily dismantle evil altars, set satanic groves on fire, and destroy every work of darkness in operation. Thus, a believer that is fasting and praying, will accomplish a lot more than if he only prayed.

The combination of prayer with fasting was key to victories in the outstanding lives and ministries of God's prophets in the Bible. The result of this spiritual fusion enabled men to survive horrible nights in the den of lions and overcome the heat of the seven-fold fiery furnace.

The duo of prayer and fasting easily unsettles the enemy's agenda and causes great damages to the kingdom of darkness. This becomes worse when other dimensions of prayer such as praise and thanksgiving are introduced.

Jehoshaphat's approach when he was under attack illustrates the perfect operations of this combination. As soon as he began to fast and pray, God revealed an uncommon strategy that helped him perplex his enemies and defeat their vast army.

"It came to pass after this also, that the children of Moab, and the children of Ammon, and with them other beside the Ammonites, came against Jehoshaphat to battle. Then there came some that told Jehoshaphat, saying, There cometh a great multitude against thee

from beyond the sea on this side Syria; and, behold, they be in Hazazontamar, which is Engedi.

And Jehoshaphat feared, and set himself to seek the LORD, and proclaimed a fast throughout all Judah. (2 Chronicles 20: 1-3).

"And when he had consulted with the people, he appointed singers unto the LORD, and that should praise the beauty of holiness, as they went out before the army, and to say, Praise the LORD; for his mercy endureth forever. And when they began to sing and to praise, the LORD set ambushments against the children of Ammon, Moab, and mount Seir, which were come against Judah; and they were smitten. For the children of Ammon and Moab stood up against the inhabitants of mount Seir, utterly to slay and destroy them: and when they had made an end of the inhabitants of Seir, everyone helped to destroy another." (2 Chronicles 20: 21-23).

Some of the most successful people in the Bible were neither rich, educated nor had royal upbringing. But one thing was common to them. They deeply feared God and knew how to fast and pray. As a result, they exceled in wisdom, and were tremendously used by God.

Moses was one of those characters. His selfless sacrifices won him regular slots before God. No wonder, God spoke with him often as a man speaks with his friend. By the same token, apostle Paul survived several tragedies because he was a man of prayer and fasting.

Fasting enables the soul to be emptied of all worldliness, creating room for the infilling with the Spirit and the word of God. That way, God's purpose is revealed to the natural man. And when he prays, he will not pray amiss because he is praying the will of God.

Before Elijah showed himself to King Ahab, to reverse the three and a half years of drought and famine in Israel, he prepared himself by fasting and praying. Even though he was on God's assignment, he did not take that for granted.

"So Ahab went up to eat and to drink. And Elijah went up to the top of Carmel; and he cast himself down upon the earth, and put his face between his knees, And said to his servant, Go up now, look toward the sea. And he went up, and looked, and said, There is nothing. And he said, Go again seven times. And it came to pass at the seventh time, that he said, Behold, there ariseth a little cloud out of the sea, like a man's hand. And he said, Go up, say unto Ahab, Prepare thy chariot, and get thee down that the rain stop thee not. And it came to pass in the meanwhile, that the heaven was black with clouds and wind, and there was a great rain. And Ahab rode and went to Jezreel." (1 Kings 18: 42-45).

After Elijah disgraced all the prophets of Ball on Mount Carmel, he asked King Ahab to go and eat. But he remained on that mountain top and prayed until he heard the sound of abundance of rain. All the while, he ate nothing.

When a child of God that knows his rights in Christ fasts and prays with the proper motive, he will cause things to happen in the spirit realm that will influence conditions on the natural sphere. Prophet Elijah was such a man, and his life reflected the great power of fasting and prayer.

Fasting and prayer are the metaphorical spiritual grease that fast track the wheels of miracles. Once they mount the platform of faith, the blind begins to see, the deaf hear, the heavens release their rain, and the barren receive strength to conceive and bring forth children.

It is God's joy to see his children operate at high spiritual dimensions of power. Fasting and prayer inspires this manifestation of God's image in the natural man. Jesus performed all his miracles because he knew the benefits received when a person combines his fasting with prayer.

Thus, any a Christian who will boldly combine the art of prayer with a holy fast will literally walk on water and silence storms. That is why the enemy respects Christians who fast and pray regularly. This powerful combination is his worst nightmare.

When righteous prayer is combined with genuine fast, based on the scriptures, God's will is readily revealed and clearly understood. God easily makes his plans known to those who in total humility and faith, sacrificially seek his face.

"Lord, have mercy on my son: for he is lunatick, and sore vexed: for ofttimes he falleth into the fire, and oft into the water. And I brought him to thy disciples, and they could not cure him. Then Jesus answered and said, O faithless and perverse generation, how long shall I be with you? how long shall I suffer you? bring him hither to me. And Jesus rebuked the devil; and he departed out of him: and the child was cured from that very hour" *(Matthew 17: 15- 18).*

"Then came the disciples to Jesus apart, and said, Why could not we cast him out? And Jesus said unto them, Because of your unbelief: for verily I say unto you, If ye have faith as a grain of mustard seed, ye shall say unto this mountain, Remove hence to yonder place; and it shall remove; and nothing shall be impossible unto you. Howbeit this kind goeth not out but by prayer and fasting". (Matthew 17: 19-21)

In the above case, Jesus used the healing of a young lad to explain the benefits and power of fasting. While he admitted the inevitability of prayer over many cases, he pointed to the necessity of fasting without which tougher issues will remain unresolved.

He explained that victories over tough situations only come with prior sacrifice and readiness. Prayer is something a believer can do anytime and anywhere. But this is not so with the discipline of fasting, which demands readiness ahead of time.

A Christian that is used to regular fasting cannot be ambushed in any situation. He is always ready to confront challenges because he has a supernatural advantage having prepared ahead. Therefore, no spiritual or natural problems can contend with him.

Through prayer and fasting, a righteous child of God can appeal to his unfailing compassion and remind him of his promises. The scriptures reveal that God will not turn away anyone who honestly sets his affections on spiritual standards. (Colossians 3: 1-5)

Prayer generally speaks to the hand of God, seeking for what it can receive. But a holy fast with prayer speaks to God's heart, expressing the desire for friendship seeking for fellowship with him and searching the depth of his riches. (Romans 11: 33).

Some problems are so difficult to deal with that no power on earth can handle them. But with God, nothing is impossible. So, while prayer seeks the hand of God that makes all things, fasting appeals to his heart that makes all things possible.

In that mode, a believer can literally move mountains, brake chains of brass, cut bars of iron asunder, and cause things that did not exist to come into being as if they existed before. And that is when the redeemed of the Lord, even in their weakness can clearly hear God speaking.

The God approved fasting and prayer connects the believer's spirit to the spirit of God in whose image he is made. That is when the power to do exploits for God, and to work signs, miracles and wonders is unleashed upon that Christian.

Thus, fasting and prayer form the best spiritual alliance a believer can readily rely on for spiritual revival. For while the fast gradually weakens the flesh, prayer essentially lifts the human spirit into the holy hill where it is filled with godly strength.

When a believer's fast and prayers are focused on God by simple, but unswerving faith, God will meet that person at the specific point of his petition. Thus, fasting and prayer enjoy that spiritual privilege that easily attracts divine attention to problems.

A Christian who regularly fasts and prays the word of God word will certainly attract heaven's attention. He will receive responses that are in the perfect will of God.

He will also have peace of mind, even when the answer is not favorable.

Praying and fasting will save a soul from the urge to rebel against God and his word. Because there is no time to fall for distractions, there will be no room to commit sin which is what separates believers from God.

A believer who fasts and prays regularly will not engage in frivolities. His mind is focused on his objectives, his studying of the Bible and meditations. So, he has no time to spare on gossips, envy, or pride.

Rather, he spends his valuable time appreciating God for his innumerable goodness. It is great time to show gratitude to God for great and meagre things. It is an appropriate time to surrender your battles to God and to intercede for your family and friends.

It is not a time to murmur, dispute or to grumble as there is no wiggle-room for these vices. But it is a time to praise God and glorify him for his grace and mercies. And to exult God for the price he paid to redeem you from bondage. (Philippians 2: 14-16).

We live in a perverse society filled with violence and unrelenting cruelty whose odor of filthiness, decay and decadence will soon incur the righteous indignation of God. The sins of this generation have become worse than that of the men of Sodom and Gomorrah.

The holy God demands a high level of holiness from all his faithful children. His eyes are so pure, they cannot behold iniquity. That is one reason the Bible encourages the attitude of fasting and prayer as a good way of avoiding God's wrath and for preparing for the return of Christ.

PRAYER POINTS

1. My father, in this fasting program, let my prayers evoke the sound of abundance of rain of miracles, in Jesus' name.

2. My father, as I fast and pray, bless me according to your mercy and not because of my righteousness, in Jesus' name.

3. O Lord, as I fast and pray, create in me a new heart, and renew a right spirit withing me, in Jesus' name.

4. As I fast and pray, every witchcraft register containing my name, burn to ashes, in Jesus' name.

5. Thunder of God, as I fast and pray, answer for me on any evil altar evoking my name, in Jesus' name.

6. As I fast and pray, let destiny wasters delegated to waste my destiny be wasted, in Jesus' name.

7. As I fast and pray, let powers that have sworn to keep me in captivity, drown, in Jesus' name.

8. As I fast and pray, let all ancestral limitations attached to my destiny be detached, in Jesus' name.

9. As I fast and pray, let powers that abort testimonies in my life, receive double destruction, in Jesus' name.

10. As I fast and pray, let star hunters monitoring my star become permanently blind, in Jesus' name.

11. My father, as I fast and pray, forgive the iniquities of my ancestors, and have compassion on me, in Jesus' name.

12. O God, do exceeding abundantly, more than I can ask or think, as I fast and pray, in Jesus' name.

13. Holy Spirit, remove everything in me that is not of God, as I fast and pray, in Jesus' name.

14. My father, let your word transform my life, as I fast and pray, in Jesus' name.

CHAPTER ELEVEN

BENEFITS OF FASTING AND PRAYER

THE CONCEPT OF FASTING IS MENTIONED ABOUT SEVENTY times in the Bible, and its rewards are fully documented there. In the book of Prophet Isaiah, we can find several conditions that define a God approved fast and the benefits attached to a genuine fasting and prayer program (Isaiah 58: 3-12).

Every session of fasting and prayers by a believer represents a declaration of total dependence on God. God is always delighted at such form of worship and in response, he unleashes his unreserved blessings upon those who engage in them.

These sacred processes provide the best platform for believers to build righteous spiritual life in Christ. Such believers eventually become assets to the kingdom of God. These are the ones that the Devil respects because he understands the source of their power.

But though these weapons can bind or loose the Devil and destroy his evil works, they are only accessible to those whose ways are right with God. No sinner can access or operate in the power of God. The fasts and prayers of the unrighteous are abomination to God.

Everyone who will reap from the benefits of a fast must conform to standards of divine integrity. The Devil will hurt any sinner who attempts to exploit the promises of God. And any form of godlessness will give him the right to do so.

All promises of God are tied to obeying the terms of his covenant. The blessings of fasting and prayer are not excluded. Certain terms must be fulfilled before anyone can receive these benefits. In 2 Chronicles, four of such conditions and three blessings are clearly stated.

"If my people, which are called by my name, shall humble themselves, and pray, and seek my face, and turn from their wicked ways; then will I hear from heaven, and will forgive their sin, and will heal their land." (2 Chronicles 7: 14).

Thus, the benefits of fasting and prayer can be appropriated by the deliberate choice to obey the conditions stated in God's word. The terms in the scripture above include humility (which implies fasting), fervent prayer, seeking God's face and repentance from sins.

Fasting humbles the soul. And according to God's word, humility is a condition for receiving his promises. The scriptures say that God hears their prayers, forgives their sins, and heals their land. Thus, God favors all those who fast because this humbles the soul.

When believers fast and pray, God is pleased and he honors them, especially when their motives are right. A soul that will come before God must be spiritually transformable. It is under this condition that God's spirit will unite with the human spirit to change that life for good.

Again, there is no one alive who has never experienced the feeling of tiredness. Strong men even get weak and wearied in their spirit just as in their flesh. But weakness is not always wrong before God. Because it is when the Christian is weak that he can completely rely on God.

"And he said unto me, My grace is sufficient for thee: for my strength is made perfect in weakness. Most gladly therefore will I rather glory in my infirmities, that the power of Christ may rest upon me. Therefore, I take pleasure in infirmities, in reproaches, in necessities, in persecutions, in distresses for Christ's sake: for when I am weak, then am I strong" (2 Corinthians 12: 9-10).

So, fasting and prayer teach the surrendered Christian, humbled by lack and toughened by hardships, to take delight in living with infirmities and without necessities of life, for Christ's sake. It is in this condition that many lean to God for that sufficient grace which he alone provides.

The believer feels the power of God that is in him more when his is most feeble. Thus, the true strength of any Christian is a measure of what God can do through him when he cannot do anything by his own power. By fasting and prayer, a Christian can come to this point.

Fasting is one way of communicating faith in God. So, when the fragrant prayer of a faithful soul is kindled on the fiery altar of a fast, an irresistible aroma like the smoke of sweet incense, literarily rises to God. This is a wonderful way of expressing trust and confidence in God

"Let my prayer be set forth before thee as incense; and the lifting up of my hands as the evening sacrifice" (Psalm 141:2).

God stands by believers who in perplexity cry to him through their fast and prayers. He knows the desires of every heart and never fails to meet each person at the very point of their needs. In some circumstances, he instantly responded with comfort and justice.

"And whiles I was speaking, and praying, and confessing my sin and the sin of my people Israel, and presenting my supplication before the LORD my God for the holy mountain of my God; Yea, whiles I was speaking in prayer, even the man Gabriel, whom I had seen in the vision at the beginning, being caused to fly swiftly, touched me about the time of the evening oblation. And he informed me, and talked with me, and said, O Daniel, I am now come forth to give thee skill and understanding. At the beginning of thy supplications the commandment came forth, and I am come to shew thee; for thou art greatly beloved: therefore understand the matter, and consider the vision" (Daniel 9; 20-23).

God always satisfies those who genuinely fast and pray regularly with blessings. That was why characters like Moses, Daniel, Elijah, and apostle Paul, were bold like the lion on the earth sphere and soared like the eagle in the spirit realm.

They were strong and did exploits because their spirits were knit with the Spirit of God. So, their souls burnt fervently with zeal and the fresh fire of revival. They did nothing by their own will but accomplished all things through Christ, their strength.

God is gracious and merciful, slow to anger and of great kindness. So, when a sinner honestly repents, confesses his sins, and returns to God with all his heart, he forgives him. Fasting, and prayer provides that right opportunity for a person to weep and mourn for his evil ways

"Therefore also now, saith the LORD, *turn ye even to me with all your heart, and with fasting, and with weeping, and with mourning: And rend your heart, and not your garments, and turn unto the* LORD *your God: for he is gracious and merciful, slow to anger, and of great kindness, and repenteth him of the evil: (Joel 2: 12).*

The body is linked with the spirit through the soul. During fasting and prayer, the physical body rests from foods enabling the spirit to align with the spirit of God. This allows for a renewal of that man's spirit and an amiable transformation of his soul by the spirit of God.

This breeds new life into the entire human body. This also allows the organs to be detoxified of poisons. And with this regeneration of the spirit the whole being becomes an undefiled instrument, preserved and worthy of presentation to God as a living sacrifice (Romans 12:1).

"He giveth power to the faint; and to them that have no might he increaseth strength. Even the youths shall faint and be weary, and the young men shall utterly fall: But they that wait upon the LORD *shall renew their strength; they shall mount up with wings as eagles; they*

shall run, and not be weary; and they shall walk, and not faint." (Isaiah 40: 29-31).

When the human soul is right with God, it becomes easy for his spirit to venture into the spirit realm and access supernatural power. This is where the power for the miraculous resides. That is why those who wait on God in prayer and fasting readily operate at this dimension.

The sacrifice of fasting is a trusted process that lifts the soul to the spiritual dimension where battles are fought. This is where serious problems that require serious attention are dealt with and where souls in bondage are disentangled from their chains.

That is why the sacred religious fasting must be considered as a mandate and not just an option or suggestion. It is no wonder that most characters in the Bible considered as God's Generals understood this secret and they employed it.

A person who fasts regularly will always be on "spiritual fire". His life is secure in Christ and the Devil cannot take him by surprise. Regular times in God's presence strengthen the believer's muscles and provide him with the necessary power to mount up with wings like the eagle.

A righteous mind has no value for what the enemy offers and will not be available to the Devil. Such virtuous habit can only be developed through persistent prayer and fasting during which time a Christian also masters his unique way of hearing from God.

The Christian who meaningfully fasts and regularly too, will attain a level of spiritual consciousness that will bring his sense of imagination in line with the will of God.

This will keep him away from settling for less than what God has offered him.

Fasting and prayer will make a man's soul hungry to do what is delightful to Jesus. And the more of Christ that Christian pursues and acquires, the more like him he becomes. It is at this level in life, that most Christians become instruments of signs and wonders in God's hand.

A Christian who fasts and prays regularly will appreciate God's kingdom principles better than the believer who does not. He is certain to operate at higher spiritual dimensions where he easily accesses the benefits of supernatural power and accomplishes tougher tasks with ease.

A combined fast with fiery prayers is the best platform for altering conditions both on the physical and in spirit realms. It enables a natural man to operate from the spirit realm and cause things to happen on earth sphere, which ordinarily would not be possible.

Prophet Elijah was an ordinary man with natural emotions, like all men. But at his command, heaven heard his voice and obeyed his decree. And for three years and six months, there was neither rain nor dew on the land of Israel, according to his decree.

"Elias was a man subject to like passions as we are, and he prayed earnestly that it might not rain: and it rained not on the earth by the space of three years and six months. And he prayed again, and the heaven gave rain, and the earth brought forth her fruit" (James 5: 17-18).

But after a long period of draught and famine, he reappeared before king Ahab, at the direction of God.

And having destroyed the prophets of Baal and Asherah, he remained on Mount Carmel praying for rainfall, while king Ahab went to eat and drink.

He was persistent in prayer and waited there relentlessly, eating nor drinking nothing while seeking God's favor for the rain. And he did not cease with his request until, a cloud, the size of a man's fist, appeared in the sky. That is the power of fasting with prayer.

When God created the heavens, the earth, and all things in them, it pleased him to form man in his image and likeness to rule over the works of his hand. He gave him dominion over all things including the astral powers and the elements. Elijah knew he had this power, and he used it.

Great men and women of the Bible understood that fasting was a way to accessing power from the courts of heaven. To them, fasting was a sacred time to enjoy the privileges of seeing the invisible and hearing the inaudible.

In the same way, the graces of faith, humility and total surrender give the natural man the confidence and boldness to enter the throne of mercy. Those who understand this simple secret, rule the visible world from the invisible realm.

Through fasting and prayers, hidden wells of divine knowledge, understanding and wisdom are revealed. And those who drink from these wells are blessed with power to operate at supernatural levels which are rich in God's blessings.

Believers who Fast and pray have access into God's presence and can draw incredible power from there. This is the power that is required to fulfill human purpose and accomplish works that are beyond ordinary human capacity for God's kingdom.

God wants to manifest his power to the church and to the world in very great measure. But the way he does it is by enduing willing, hungry souls who humbly fast and regularly pray on the sacred platform of faith, with this power to do exploits.

This power comes from God, but he gives it in the form of gifts to his children after they are baptized in the Holy Ghost. With this power, a Christian will serve God in uncommon ways, accomplish his will, and face life's circumstances with confidence.

Every Christian needs this power for daily guidance. The Bible is generally referred to as the good book, and its spiritual author is called the good shepherd. Surrendering the human soul to Jesus through fasting and prayer is a sign of readiness to be led as the shepherd leads his sheep.

Jesus is always knocking at the door of the believer's sinful heart waiting to be invited in for reconciliation. He is not asking anyone to fix his broken life before asking him in. He will put any man's broken pieces together when they are handed to him.

That is why, anyone that turns away from all material pursuits to let him into his life never remains the same again. He fills that soul with life-changing virtues that turn him into light to the world and salt to the earth. ((Revelation 3: 20)

Fasting and prayer bring a glow to life. This is because the devotion to the word of God and the God of the word during that time satisfies a man's hunger with God's goodness. This is what brings God's glory and causes a sense of the sweetness in his presence during a fast.

At the heart of any fast is the desire for intimacy with God. It is the motive of all fasting with prayer, and what inspires the determination to seek the face of God and to do his will. The glory of God only comes as a benefit after this is accomplished.

Fasting and prayer help clear the mind of its filth, enabling the Christian to deal with vices and emotions such as anxiety, fear, pride, and doubts. They transform the spirit and the soul and influence the flesh to hunger for qualitative spiritual life.

A regular fasting and prayer lifestyle helps to reshape the human perspective about life and Godliness. A person that fasts and prays will be close to God. And the closer a man's spirit and his soul are to God, the bigger God appears to that life.

This increases faith, builds confidence, and enables that believer to have a better perception of the greatness of the almighty God with whom nothing is impossible. A Christian who realizes the magnitude of his God will always consider all problems as conquerable.

It is God's desire to interact with the man he created in his image and likeness. This friendship occurs more as a person regularly fasts and prays. Such interactions save the human soul from being influenced by the world with the possibility of making that soul an enemy of God.

When a Christian fast's and prays, his soul is transported beyond natural boundaries into the spirit sphere where he can experience time-tested truths and learn disciplines that make him live life that is pleasant to God. By so doing, that individual becomes more like Christ.

A believer's soul in the presence of God has a better perception of his divine power, strength, and goodness. And the nearer a person is to the almighty God, the farther away he is from challenges, the smaller what seemed like unconquerable problems appear, and the weaker they become.

Closeness to God creates the confident feeling that the solution to a problem is near at hand. A believer whose focus is on God while he fasts and prays will find strength and peace from God. He will also realize that the size of his "mountain" is small compared to the size of his God.

"The LORD will give strength unto his people; the LORD will bless his people with peace" (Psalms 29: 11).

And as a person studies the Bible during this time and meditates on the word of God, his mind is rewired and the filthy, self-centered, carnal imaginations embedded there are replaced with Christ-like thoughts that put others first. This way, material thoughts are replaced godly truths.

Fasting and prayer will enable a Christian to resist the seductive substitutes which Satan offers to the carnally minded. These are his tricks for distracting righteous souls from receiving the divine blessings which God has provided for those who diligently seek him.

Meaningful fasting and prayer help reboot a believer's spiritual mindset and values. A person's spiritual life will go into limbo if he relies only on his "old anointing". Cracks that allow for ungodly thoughts to infiltrate any soul that relies on "yesterday's" anointing will develop.

But a regular program of fasting and prayer will sensitize the spirit, rekindle that soul with holy fire, keep it vigilant and restore its boldness. This will enable the child of God that is willing to pay the price to soar like the eagle.

Any Christian who engages in fasting with prayer will observe a quickening of his understanding in the word of God. This is what empowers many bold children of God to be more confident in living and acting on the power of divine promises.

Fasting and prayer enable a soul to enter the realm of "better things", explained by apostle Paul, in his epistle to the Hebrew believers. This is the realm of a better covenant, with better priests, on a better altar, with better sacrifices, offered by better faith (Hebrews 12:2).

From these platforms, a Christian can infiltrate the spirit realm and claim victories already obtained by Jesus for believers on the cross. They are sure pathways that lead to the secret spiritual bank reserved for all those who fear God and obey his commandment.

Though fasting and prayer are powerful tools for spiritual warfare, what matters most is the result they achieve. If they cannot deliver a soul from the cords of affliction or save a soul that is perishing from works of darkness, then they are worthless before God.

Although fasting can be a tough experience, especially in a society with so much to eat and drink, it has immense value for those who give it a trial. It tempers the avarice of the flesh through the deliberate control of natural foods and increases the appetite for spiritual nourishment.

A Holy Spirit inspired fast will offer clarity of vision and cause the individual to perceive, analyze and address natural events and situations from a better perspective. A person that fasts regularly will be rich in the gifts and power to do God's will.

There are daily, unseen battles in the life of every believer. And the arena where spiritual wickedness is conceived before execution is in the second heavens. Thus, all the problems a Christian will encounter in life will begin in the spirit realm.

Mankind is living in very evil times. And given that the kingdom of darkness is never ever on vacation, children of God are under constant bombardment by the enemy, especially from the activities of the restless demons and wicked, evil spirits,

The atmosphere of solitude during a fast therefore offers the best time for sobriety and vigilance in this chaotic world. This enables vital spiritual alertness and quietness which are very necessary for hearing God's voice clearly.

Fasting and prayer offer spiritual therapy to the mind. This helps to calm the distraught nerves that cause stress to the soul and body. This, in a great measure provides solutions to several, human emotional disasters and frightening conditions that overwhelm the soul.

The overall spiritual, social, and moral conducts of a believer are positively influenced as he fasts and prays. And because that person's spirit is led and guided by the Holy Spirit during this time, his mind understands God's will and his soul easily rejects anything evil.

In such brokenness, God causes all doubt and worry to lose their power. Faith replaces fear and joy overcomes sadness, causing peace to take the place of disorder. This is the kind of world man was originally formed to enjoy before Adam lost control to the Devil.

A God approved fasting and prayer program will positively impact the spiritual and natural appetites. After a fast, a believer's hunger for God's word will increase, as will his wisdom and grace. And his natural appetites for foods and worldly comforts will be greatly diminished.

"Walk in wisdom toward them that are without, redeeming the time. Let your speech be always with grace, seasoned with salt, that ye may know how ye ought to answer every man" (Colossians 4: 5-6).

This is because the rigors of a fast put to death the carnal desires of the flesh which corrupt the soul. Afflicting the soul in this manner causes a springing forth of the human spirit which all the while is being fed with the word of God.

So, spending time in fasts and prayers brings victories over serious battles. Ezra's fast was rewarded with protection and safety for him and for the returning exiles. And Daniel's fast evoked timely intervention as well as angelic reinforcement. (Ezra 8: 21-23; Daniel 10: 2-3, 12).

Principalities, powers of the air and wicked princes of Satan are always on evil duty in the second heavens. But the fasting and prayer of believers invite angelic warriors into spiritual warfare to intervene on their behalf.

Every time a believer worships God, he attracts his attention and favors, especially when the motive is right, and that believer is praying in accordance with God's will. And more benefits are received when such prayers are combined with a fast by a child of God who knows his rights.

Daniel was a great prayer warrior. But it was his combined prayer and fasts that constituted worse nightmare to his enemies because it put him in direct touch with the throne-room of God and attracted instant response from messengers of heaven.

Fasting and prayer will restore confidence, strength, courage and open doors for bodily healing. As a soul is filled with God's truth during this process, it finds it easy to release problems to God. This way, that soul finds overwhelming peace, joy, and comfort in God.

Every Christian is called into a relationship with God through the finished work of Christ on the cross. But while this intimate friendship is sustained by the Holy Ghost, each believer has a role in ensuring that God's entire plan for humanity is fulfilled through him,

God created the heavens, the earth and all that is in them without any human cooperation. In the same way, he can accomplish all his plans for mankind without human help. But the beauty of divine creation is that God designed the earth with human cooperation in mind.

Thus, he makes man's smallest inputs to matter in the perfection of his purpose by using people who sacrifice in meaningful ways to worship him. God is pleased when a person denies himself the passing pleasures of this world to find time for him.

When Abraham left his birth country and abandoned his kindred and father's house to follow God, it pleased him. Ruth the Moabitess also abandoned her people and their gods to follow the sovereign God of her mother-in-law. Such selfless acts in faith, delight God's heart.

And those Christians who readily give preference to spiritual values rather than focus on material possessions become God's hands and feet for reaching the dark world. And he blesses them with gifts that enable them to function more effectively for his kingdom.

So, through fasting and prayer, the human soul will appreciate that nothing meaningful can be achieved under the sun, except by the selfless sacrifices made by men through the Son of God. These are the things that bring justice upon the earth and joy in heaven.

Also, fasting and prayer help the human mind to obtain power and knowledge which are life-changing keys for doing God's will. God is looking for souls, not just to make them smart on earth, but to give them gifts with which to serve in his earthly kingdom.

God is honored when a Christian walks worthy of the knowledge, wisdom, understanding, and power acquired from him. Applying these traits to help the church and the world saves souls for Christ and inspires others to follow the way of faith.

PRAYER POINTS

1. My father, as I fast and pray, let me find grace to help in times of need, in Jesus' name.

2. O Lord, as I fast and pray, disappoint the instruments of torture and death reserved for me, in Jesus' name.

3. O God, as I fast and pray, turn the plans of the enemy against me upside down, in Jesus' name.

4. Holy Spirit, as I fast and pray expose and disgrace every pestilence hiding in the darkness for my sake, in Jesus' name.

5. Holy Spirit, as I fast and pray, render every spell operating in life powerless, in Jesus' name.

6. My father, as I fast and pray render my body uninhabitable to sickness and disease, in Jesus' name.

7. Holy Ghost fire, as I fast and pray, destroy every landing pad of problems in my foundation, in Jesus' name.

8. Power provoking me against the will of God, be crushed, as I fast and pray, in Jesus' name.

9. O God, defend me from the terrors of the night, as I fast and pray, in Jesus' name.

10. O Lord, as I fast and pray, shield me from the arrows that fly by day, in Jesus' name.

11. Holy Spirit, as I fast and pray, reverse every evil judgement upon my life, in Jesus' name.

12. Holy Spirit, as I fast and pray, frustrate the powers making enchantment with my names, in Jesus' name.

13. Judgement of God, fall upon my adversaries, as I fast and pray, in Jesus' name.

14. O God, as I come boldly to your throne of grace in this fasting and prayer program, answer me by fire, in Jesus' name.

Printed in the United States
by Baker & Taylor Publisher Services

Printed in the United States
by Baker & Taylor Publisher Services